STECK-VAUGHN

TABE®
Fundamentals
Focus on Skills

Applied Math

LEVEL D

2nd Edition

MAR 2017

Steck Vaughn™

HOUGHTON MIFFLIN HARCOURT
Supplemental Publishers

www.SteckVaughn.com
800-531-5015

Photo Credits: P iv: ©Bluestone Productions/SuperStock
Royalty Free; 2: ©Photodisc/Getty Images
Royalty Free; 4: ©Veer Royalty Free; 69: Corbis Royalty Free.

Reviewers

Victor Gathers
Regional Coordinator of Adult Services
New York City Department of Education
Brooklyn Adult Learning Center
Brooklyn, New York

Brannon Lentz
Assistant Director of Adult Education/Skills Training
Northwest Shoals Community College
Muscle Shoals, Alabama

Jean Pierre-Pipkin, Ed.D.
Director of Beaumont I.S.D. Adult Education
Cooperative Consortium
Beaumont, Texas

ISBN-13: 978-1-4190-5358-0
ISBN-10:   1-4190-5358-2

© 2009, 2004 Steck-Vaughn, an imprint of HMH Supplemental Publishers Inc.

Steck-Vaughn is a trademark of HMH Supplemental Publishers Inc.

TABE® is a trademark of McGraw-Hill, Inc. Such company has neither endorsed nor authorized this publication.

Printed in the United States of America.

10 11 12 0982 17 16

4500589088

Contents

To the Learner

Congratulations on your decision to study for the TABE! You are taking an important step in your educational career. This book will help you do your best on the TABE. You'll also find hints and strategies that will help you prepare for test day. Practice these skills—your success lies in your hands.

What Is the TABE?

TABE stands for the Tests of Adult Basic Education. These paper-and-pencil tests, published by McGraw-Hill, measure your progress on basic skills. There are five tests in all: Reading, Mathematics Computation, Applied Mathematics, Language, and Spelling.

TABE Levels M, D, and A

Test	Number of Items	Suggested Working Time (in minutes)
1 Reading	50	50
2 Mathematics Computation	25	15
3 Applied Mathematics	50	50
4 Language	55	39
5 Spelling	20	10

Test 1 Reading

This test measures basic reading skills. The main concepts covered by this test are word meaning, critical thinking, and understanding basic information.

Many things on this test will look familiar to you. They include documents and forms necessary to your everyday life, such as directions, bank statements, maps, and consumer labels. The test also includes items that measure your ability to find and use information from a dictionary, table of contents, or library computer display. The TABE also tests a learner's understanding of fiction and nonfiction passages.

Test 2 Mathematics Computation

Test 2 covers adding, subtracting, multiplying, and dividing. On the test you must use these skills with whole numbers, fractions, decimals, integers, and percents.

The skills covered in the Mathematics Computation test are the same skills you use daily to balance your checkbook, double a recipe, or fix your car.

Test 3 Applied Mathematics

The Applied Mathematics test links mathematical ideas to real-world situations. Many things you do every day require basic math. Making budgets, cooking, and doing your taxes all take math. The test also covers pre-algebra, algebra, and geometry. Adults need to use all these skills.

Some questions will relate to one theme. For example, auto repairs could be the subject and the question could focus on the repair schedule. You may be told when a car was last repaired and how often it needs to be repaired. You might have to predict the next maintenance date.

Many of the items will not require you to use a specific strategy or formula to get the correct answer. Instead this test challenges you to use your own problem-solving strategies to answer the question.

Test 4 Language

The Language test asks you to analyze different types of writing. Examples are business letters, resumes, job reports, and essays. For each task, you have to show you understand good writing skills.

The questions fit adult interests and concerns. Some questions ask you to think about what is wrong in the written material. In other cases, you will correct sentences and paragraphs.

Test 5 Spelling

In everyday life, you need to spell correctly, especially in the workplace. The spelling words on this test are words that many people misspell and words that are commonly used in adult writing.

Test-Taking Tips

1. Read the directions very carefully. Make sure you read through them word for word. If you are not sure what the question says, ask the person giving the test to explain it to you.

2. Read each question carefully. Make sure you know what it means and what you have to do.

3. Read all of the answers carefully, even if you think you know the answer.

4. Make sure that the reading supports your answer. Don't answer without checking the reading. Don't rely only on outside knowledge.

5. Answer all of the questions. If you can't find the right answer, rule out the answers that you know are wrong. Then try to figure out the right answer. If you still don't know, make your best guess.

6. If you can't figure out the answer, put a light mark by the question and come back to it later. Erase your marks before you finish.

7. Don't change an answer unless you are sure your first answer is wrong. Usually your first idea is the correct answer.

8. If you get nervous, stop for a while. Take a few breaths and relax. Then start working again.

How to Use *TABE Fundamentals*

Step-by-Step Instruction In Levels M and D, each lesson starts with step-by-step instruction on a skill. The instruction contains examples and then a test example with feedback. This instruction is followed by practice questions. Work all of the questions in the lesson's practice and then check your work in the Answers and Explanations in the back of the book.

The Level A books contain practice for each skill covered on the TABE. Work all of the practice questions and then check your work in the Answers and Explanations in the back of the book.

Reviews The lessons in Levels M and D are grouped by a TABE Objective. At the end of each TABE Objective, there is a Review. Use these Reviews to find out if you need to review any of the lessons before continuing.

Performance Assessment At the end of every book, there is a special section called the Performance Assessment. This section is similar to the TABE test. It has the same number and type of questions. This assessment will give you an idea of what the real test is like.

Answer Sheet At the back of the book is a practice bubble-in answer sheet. Practice bubbling in your answers. Fill in the answer sheet carefully. For each answer, mark only one numbered space on the answer sheet. Mark the space beside the number that corresponds to the question. Mark only one answer per question. On the real TABE, if you have more than one answer per question, they will be scored as incorrect. Be sure to erase any stray marks.

Strategies and Hints Pay careful attention to the TABE Strategies and Hints throughout this book. Strategies are test-taking tips that help you do better on the test. Hints give you extra information about a skill.

Setting Goals

On the following page is a form to help you set your goals. Setting goals will help you get more from your work in this book.

Section 1. Why do you want to do well on the TABE? Take some time now to set your short-term and long-term goals on page 3.

Section 2. Making a schedule is one way to set priorities. Deadlines will help you stay focused on the steps you need to take to reach your goals.

Section 3. Your goals may change over time. This is natural. After a month, for example, check the progress you've made. Do you need to add new goals or make any changes to the ones you have? Checking your progress on a regular basis helps you reach your goals.

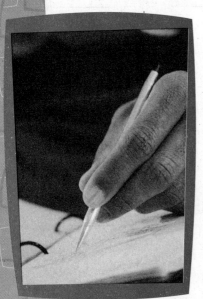

For more information on setting goals, see Steck-Vaughn's *Start Smart Goal Setting Strategies*.

1. Set Your Goals

What is your long-term goal for using this book?

_____

_____

_____

Complete these areas to identify the smaller steps to take to reach your long-term goal.

Content area	What I Know	What I Want to Learn
Reading	_____	_____
Language	_____	_____
Spelling	_____	_____
Math	_____	_____
Other	_____	_____

2. Make a Schedule

Set some deadlines for yourself.

> For a 20-week planning calendar, see Steck-Vaughn's *Start Smart Planner*.

Goals	Begin Date	End Date
_____	_____	_____
_____	_____	_____
_____	_____	_____
_____	_____	_____
_____	_____	_____

3. Celebrate Your Success

Note the progress you've made. If you made changes in your goals, record them here.

_____

_____

_____

_____

To the Instructor

About TABE

The Tests of Adult Basic Education are designed to meet the needs of adult learners in ABE programs. Written and designed to be relevant to adult learners' lives and interests, this material focuses on the life, job, academic, and problem-solving skills that the typical adult needs.

Because of the increasing importance of thinking skills in any curriculum, *TABE Fundamentals* focuses on critical thinking throughout each TABE Objective.

The TABE identifies the following thinking processes as essential to learning and achieving goals in daily life:

- ✦ Gather Information
- ✦ Organize Information
- ✦ Analyze Information
- ✦ Generate Ideas
- ✦ Synthesize Elements
- ✦ Evaluate Outcomes

Test 1 Reading

The TABE measures an adult's ability to understand home, workplace, and academic texts. The ability to construct meaning from prose and visual information is also covered through reading and analyzing diagrams, maps, charts, forms, and consumer materials.

Test 2 Mathematics Computation

This test covers whole numbers, decimals, fractions, integers, percents, and algebraic expressions. Skills are carefully targeted to the appropriate level of difficulty.

Test 3 Applied Mathematics

This test emphasizes problem-solving and critical-thinking skills, with a focus on the life-skill applications of mathematics. Estimation and pattern-recognition skills also are important on this test.

Test 4 Language

The Language test focuses on writing and effective communication. Students examine writing samples that need revision, with complete-sentence and paragraph contexts for the various items. The test emphasizes editing, proofreading, and other key skills. The context of the questions are real-life settings appropriate to adults.

Test 5 Spelling

This test focuses on the words learners most typically misspell. In this way, the test identifies the spelling skills learners most need in order to communicate effectively. Items typically present high-frequency words in short sentences.

Uses of the TABE

There are three basic uses of the TABE:

Instructional

From an instructional point of view, the TABE allows instructors to assess students' entry levels as they begin an adult program. The TABE also allows instructors to diagnose learners' strengths and weaknesses in order to determine appropriate areas to focus instruction. Finally the TABE allows instructors and institutions to monitor learners' progress.

Administrative

The TABE allows institutions to assess classes in general and measure the effectiveness of instruction and whether learners are making progress.

Governmental

The TABE provides a means of assessing a school's or program's effectiveness.

The National Reporting System (NRS) and the TABE

Adult education and literacy programs are federally funded and thus accountable to the federal government. The National Reporting System monitors adult education. Developed with the help of adult educators, the NRS sets the reporting requirements for adult education programs around the country. The information collected by the NRS is used to assess the effectiveness of adult education programs and make necessary improvements.

A key measure defined by the NRS is educational gain, which is an assessment of the improvement in learners' reading, writing, speaking, listening, and other skills during their instruction. Programs assess educational gain at every stage of instruction.

NRS Functioning Levels	Grade Levels	TABE (7–8) scaled scores
Beginning ABE Literacy	0–1.9	Reading . . . . 367 and below Total Math . . . . 313 and below Language . . . . . 392 and below
Beginning Basic Education	2–3.9	Reading . . . . 368–460 Total Math . . . . 314–441 Language 393–490
Low Intermediate Basic Education	4–5.9	Reading . . . . 461–517 Total Math . . . . 442–505 Language 491–523
High Intermediate Basic Education	6–8.9	Reading . . . . 518–566 Total Math . . . . 506–565 Language 524–559
Low Adult Secondary Education	9–10.9	Reading . . . . 567–595 Total Math . . . . 566–594 Language 560–585

According to the NRS guidelines, states select the method of assessment appropriate for their needs. States can assess educational gain either through standardized tests or through performance-based assessment. Among the standardized tests typically used under NRS guidelines is the TABE, which meets the NRS standards both for administrative procedures and for scoring.

The three main methods used by the NRS to collect data are the following:

1. **Direct program reporting,** from the moment of student enrollment
2. **Local follow-up surveys,** involving learners' employment or academic goals
3. **Data matching,** or sharing data among agencies serving the same clients so that outcomes unique to each program can be identified.

Two of the major goals of the NRS are academic achievement and workplace readiness. Educational gain is a means to reaching these goals. As learners progress through the adult education curriculum, the progress they make should help them either obtain or keep employment or obtain a diploma, whether at the secondary school level or higher. The TABE is flexible enough to meet both the academic and workplace goals set forth by the NRS.

Using *TABE Fundamentals*

Adult Basic Education Placement

From the outset, the TABE allows effective placement of learners. You can use the *TABE Fundamentals* series to support instruction of those skills where help is needed.

High School Equivalency

Placement often involves predicting learners' success on the GED, the high school equivalency exam. Each level of *TABE Fundamentals* covers Reading, Language, Spelling, Applied and Computational Math to allow learners to focus their attention where it is needed.

Assessing Progress

Each TABE skill is covered in a lesson. These lessons are grouped by TABE Objective. At the end of each TABE Objective, there is a Review. Use these Reviews to find out if the learners need to review any of the skills before continuing.

At the end of the book, there is a special section called the Performance Assessment. This section is similar to the TABE test. It has the same number and type of questions. You can use the Performance Assessment as a timed pretest or posttest with your learners, or as a more general review for the actual TABE.

Steck-Vaughn's *TABE Fundamentals* Program at a Glance

The charts on the following page provide a quick overview of the elements of Steck-Vaughn's *TABE Fundamentals* series. Use this chart to match the TABE objectives with the skill areas for each level. This chart will come in handy whenever you need to find which objectives fit the specific skill areas you need to cover.

Steck-Vaughn's *TABE Fundamentals* Program at a Glance

TABE OBJECTIVE	Level M		Level D		Level A
	Reading	Language and Spelling	Reading	Language and Spelling	Reading, Language, and Spelling
Reading					
Interpret Graphic Information	◆		◆		◆
Words in Context	◆		◆		◆
Recall Information	◆		◆		◆
Construct Meaning	◆		◆		◆
Evaluate/Extend Meaning	◆		◆		◆
Language					
Usage		◆		◆	◆
Sentence Formation		◆		◆	◆
Paragraph Development		◆		◆	◆
Punctuation and Capitalization		◆		◆	◆
Writing Convention		◆		◆	◆
Spelling					
Vowel		◆		◆	◆
Consonant		◆		◆	◆
Structural Unit		◆		◆	◆

TABE OBJECTIVE	Level M		Level D		Level A
	Math Computation	Applied Math	Math Computation	Applied Math	Computational and Applied Math
Mathematics Computation					
Addition of Whole Numbers	◆				
Subtraction of Whole Numbers	◆				
Multiplication of Whole Numbers	◆		◆		
Division of Whole Numbers	◆		◆		
Decimals	◆		◆		◆
Fractions	◆		◆		◆
Integers			◆		◆
Percents			◆		◆
Orders of Operation			◆		◆
Applied Mathematics					
Number and Number Operations		◆		◆	◆
Computation in Context		◆		◆	◆
Estimation		◆		◆	◆
Measurement		◆		◆	◆
Geometry and Spatial Sense		◆		◆	◆
Data Analysis		◆		◆	◆
Statistics and Probability		◆		◆	◆
Patterns, Functions, Algebra		◆		◆	◆
Problem Solving and Reasoning		◆		◆	◆

Lesson 1 Recognizing Numbers

Numbers can be expressed in various ways, with numerals, with words, and with a combination of words and numerals. Numbers can also be expressed using parentheses to group them. On the TABE you will see numbers written in different forms.

Example What are some ways to show 406?

Step 1. Think of some ways to show or name numbers.

in standard form	406
as addition	400 + 6
in words	four hundred six
in numerals and words	4 hundred 6

Step 2. Numbers can also be shown by their place values. Set up a place-value chart and find the value of each digit. Add the place value of each digit to show another form.

hundreds	tens	ones
100s	10s	1s
4	0	6

The 6 means 6 ones, or **6 × 1**
The 0 means no tens, or **0 × 10**
The 4 means 4 hundreds, or **4 × 100**

$$4 \times 100 + 0 \times 10 + 6 \times 1 = 406$$

Step 3. To make this form easier to read, you can group the numbers being multiplied in parentheses. Because $0 \times 10 = 0$, you don't have to include it.

$$(4 \times 100) + (6 \times 1)$$

To check to be sure you've grouped the numbers correctly, solve the operation in the parentheses first, then add.

$$(4 \times 100) = 400$$
$$(6 \times 1) = \underline{+ 6}$$
$$406$$

Another form of 406 is $(4 \times 100) + (6 \times 1)$.

Test Example

Read the question. Circle the answer.

1   Sound travels at one thousand five hundred thirty-one meters per second while passing through salt water. Which of the following choices shows the same number?

A	153	C	1,351
B	1,531	D	1,135

1 B is one thousand five hundred thirty-one. Option A is one hundred fifty-three. Option C is one thousand three hundred fifty-one, and option D is one thousand one hundred thirty-five.

Practice

Read the question. Circle the answer.

1 Which of these numbers is four hundred eight thousand two hundred fifty-six?

A 480,256

B 48,256

C 408,256

D 482,560

2 Which of these is another way to show 307?

F three hundred seven

G 30 + 7

H $(3 \times 100) + (7 \times 10)$

J 3 hundreds 7 tens

3 The driving distance from New York to Los Angeles is two thousand seven hundred ninety-seven miles. Which number shows this distance?

A 2,979

B 2,727

C 2,779

D 2,797

4 Which is another way to show 840?

F eight hundred four

G $(8 \times 100) + (4 \times 10)$

H 4 hundred 80 four

J 800 + 4

5 A cable company has 50,093 customers. What is another way to show this number?

A fifty thousand ninety-three

B fifty thousand nine hundred three

C fifty-nine thousand three

D thirty-nine thousand fifty

6 Which of these is another way to show 407?

F four hundred seven

G $(4 \times 100) + (7 \times 10)$

H 40 + 7

J four hundreds seven tens

TABE Strategy

Four-digit numbers are written with a comma on the TABE.

Check your answers on page 122.

Place Value

Which is larger 372.5 or 37.25? The decimal point changes the value of the digits and makes the numbers different. A place value table shows this change in the values of the digit.

Hundreds	Tens	Ones	Decimal Point	Tenths	Hundredths
3	7	2	.	5	
	3	7	.	2	5

On the TABE test, you will determine the value of a digit based on its place.

Example **Use a place value chart to find the value of a digit. What is the value of the 6 in 840.16?**

Step 1. Write each digit of 840.16 in the correct place in a place value chart. The chart shows the value of each digit in the number.

Hundreds	Tens	Ones	Decimal Point	Tenths	Hundredths
8	4	0	.	1	6

Step 2. Use the place value chart to determine the value of each digit.

The 8 is in the hundreds place.   Its value is 8 hundreds, or 8×100.
The 4 is in the tens place.   Its value is 4 tens, or 4×10.
The 0 is in the ones place.   Its value is 0 ones, of 0×1.

The 1 is in the tenths place.   Its value is 1 tenth, or $1 \times \dfrac{1}{10}$.

The 6 is in the hundredths place. Its value is 6 hundredths, or $6 \times \dfrac{1}{100}$.

The value of the digit 6 in 840.16 is $\dfrac{6}{100}$.

Test Example

Read the question. Circle the answer.

1 What does the 7 in 2,813.74 mean?

 A 70

 B 7

 C $\dfrac{7}{10}$

 D $\dfrac{7}{100}$

Hint

The decimal point always appears between the ones and the tenths places.

1 C $\frac{7}{10}$ In the number 2,813.74, the 7 appears in the tenths place. The 7 stands for $7 \times \frac{1}{10}$, or $\frac{7}{10}$. Option A shows the 7 in the tens place. Option B shows the 7 in the ones place. Option D shows the 7 in the hundredths place.

Practice

Read the question. Circle the answer.

1 What does the 4 in 1,842.69 mean?

A 400

B 40

C 4

D $\frac{4}{10}$

2 What does the 5 in 913.25 mean?

F 50

G 5

H $\frac{5}{10}$

J $\frac{5}{100}$

3 Which number shows a 2 in the hundreds place?

A 21.7

B 283.9

C 829.3

D 12.47

4 Which number shows a 6 in the tenths place?

F 813.96

G 15.62

H 936.41

J 72.06

5 Which number shows a 5 in the hundredths place?

A 65.19

B 47.52

C 3.056

D 482.5

6 What does the 4 in 9,438 mean?

F 4,000

G 400

H $\frac{4}{10}$

J $\frac{4}{100}$

7 What does the 7 in 27.15 mean?

F 70

G 7

H $\frac{7}{10}$

J $\frac{7}{100}$

8 Which number shows a 1 in the hundreds place?

F 2,193

G 517.96

H 901.23

J 7,215.6

Check your answers on page 122.

Comparison

You compare amounts every day. For example, when you want to choose the best hitter on a baseball team, you probably compare batting averages. This lesson will help you compare decimals and fractions on the TABE.

Example The batting averages for four players are 0.358, 0.338, 0.372, and 0.368. Which batting average is the highest?

Step 1. Write all the numbers in a column, lining up the numbers by the decimal points. Compare the numbers in each column. The ones column has all 0s, and the tenths column has all 3s.

Step 2. Compare the numbers in the next column to the right. Because 7 is the greatest number in the column, you don't need to compare the numbers in the next column. 0.372 is the highest batting average.

0.358
0.338
0.372
0.368

0.358
0.338
0.372
0.368

The highest batting average is 0.372.

Example Four friends joined a weight-loss program. Mike lost $\frac{1}{2}$ kilogram, Tara lost $\frac{1}{3}$ kilogram, Simone lost $\frac{1}{4}$ kilogram, and Jake lost $\frac{3}{4}$ kilogram. Place the amounts they lost in order from least to greatest.

Step 1. Draw the fractions.

This shows $\frac{1}{2}$ kilogram, or how much Mike lost.

This shows $\frac{1}{3}$ kilogram, or how much Tara lost.

This shows $\frac{1}{4}$ kilogram, or how much Simone lost.

This shows $\frac{3}{4}$ kilogram, or how much Jake lost.

Step 2. Compare the shaded areas. Which bar has the least shading? Simone's bar should come first. Which bar is second? Third? Which bar has the most shading?

The amounts lost from least to greatest were $\frac{1}{4}$, $\frac{1}{3}$, $\frac{1}{2}$, and $\frac{3}{4}$ kilograms.

Example Compare $\frac{1}{3}$ and $\frac{3}{2}$ by determining if each fraction is less than or greater than 1.

Step 1. Look at the top number of the fraction $\frac{1}{3}$. If the top number is smaller than the bottom number, the fraction is less than 1.

Step 2. Look at the top number of the fraction $\frac{3}{2}$. If the top number is greater than the bottom number, the fraction is greater than 1.

$\frac{1}{3}$ is less than 1. $\frac{3}{2}$ is greater than 1. Therefore, $\frac{3}{2}$ is greater than $\frac{1}{3}$.

Test Example

Read the question. Circle the answer.

1 To make Chicken with Lemon Sauce, the cafeteria cook needs $\frac{6}{4}$ cups chicken stock, $\frac{1}{4}$ cup parsley, $\frac{1}{2}$ cup lemon juice, and $\frac{3}{4}$ cup of chopped onions. Which ingredient amount is greater than 1 cup?

A lemon juice C chicken stock

B parsley D onions

TABE Strategy

When reading fractions, read the top and bottom numbers carefully before you choose an answer.

1 **C** Chicken stock, $\frac{6}{4}$ cups. Its amount is the only one in which the top number of the fraction is larger than its bottom number.

Practice

Read the question. Circle the answer.

1 Which of these decimals is less than 0.638 and greater than 0.621?

A 0.649

B 0.613

C 0.635

D 0.620

2 Place the fractions in order from least to greatest.

$$\frac{7}{8}, \frac{9}{7}, \frac{3}{5}, \frac{7}{6}, \frac{3}{4}$$

F $\frac{3}{4}, \frac{3}{5}, \frac{7}{6}, \frac{7}{8}, \frac{9}{7}$ H $\frac{3}{5}, \frac{3}{4}, \frac{7}{8}, \frac{7}{6}, \frac{9}{7}$

G $\frac{3}{5}, \frac{3}{4}, \frac{7}{6}, \frac{7}{8}, \frac{9}{7}$ J $\frac{9}{7}, \frac{7}{6}, \frac{7}{8}, \frac{3}{4}, \frac{3}{5}$

3 The precipitation amount for New York City on April 1, 2002, was 0.69 inches. On the same day in 2003, 0.76 inches was recorded. Which amount would be greater than the 2002 total, but less than the 2003 amount?

A 0.84

B 0.77

C 0.68

D 0.74

Check your answers on page 122.

A store is having a "50% off" sale. Another store is having a similar sale but their sign says "$\frac{1}{2}$ off sale." The fraction $\frac{1}{2}$ is the same as 50%, so you know that you'll save the same at each store.

Example Jeff has painted 6 of the 10 rooms in his house. In simplest terms, what fraction of the rooms in his house has Jeff painted?

Step 1. Set up a fraction, $\frac{6}{10}$. Find a number that will go into, or divide, both 6 and 10 evenly. Since there are three 2s in 6 (or $3 \times 2 = 6$) and five 2s in 10 (or $5 \times 2 = 10$), we can say that 2 will go into, or divide, both 6 and 10 evenly.

Step 2. Reduce the fraction by dividing the top number and the bottom number by 2.

$$\frac{6}{10} \div \frac{2}{2} = \frac{3}{5}$$

Step 3. Can the fraction be reduced any more? No, because there is no number that can divide both 3 and 5 evenly. The fraction is in its simplest form.

Jeff has painted $\frac{3}{5}$ of the rooms in his house.

Example About 20% of the air you breathe is oxygen. What fraction of the air is oxygen?

Step 1. Write 20% as a fraction. Because "%" means "out of 100 parts," you can convert the 20% to a fraction by deleting the percent sign and putting 20 over 100.

$$20\% = \frac{20}{100}$$

Step 2. Reduce 20/100. Find a number that will divide both 20 and 100 evenly. Because there is one **20** in 20 and there are five **20**s in 100, divide 20 and 100 by 20.

$$\frac{20}{100} \div \frac{20}{20} = \frac{1}{5}$$

$\frac{1}{5}$ of the air you breathe is oxygen.

Test Example

1   A state park saw 30% more families visit this year than last year. What fraction shows how many more families visited the park this year?

   A $\frac{3}{10}$

   B $\frac{1}{3}$

   C $\frac{3}{33}$

   D $\frac{5}{20}$

Hint

Can the top and bottom number be divided by the same number? If so, then the fraction can be reduced.

1 **A** Write 30% as a fraction. Find a number that will divide 30 and 100 evenly. Then divide.

$$\frac{30}{100} \div \frac{10}{10} = \frac{3}{10}$$

This diagram shows the plans for a new football stadium. Study the diagram. Then do number 1.

1 What fractional part of the east section of the football stadium will have luxury seating?

A $\frac{1}{3}$

B $\frac{1}{6}$

C $\frac{1}{4}$

D $\frac{1}{2}$

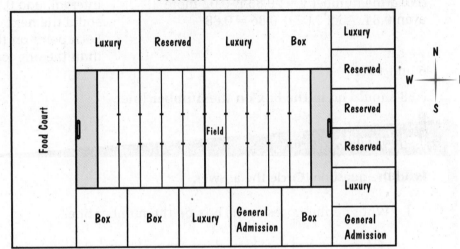

Football Stadium

This map shows the roads in Albertson. Study the map. Then do number 2.

2 The length of Netz Place is what fraction of the length of Willets Road?

F $\frac{1}{2}$

G $\frac{1}{3}$

H $\frac{1}{4}$

J $\frac{1}{5}$

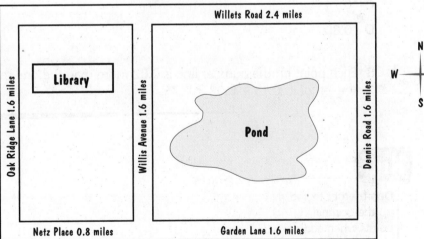

Map of Albertson

Check your answers on page 122.

Lesson 5 · Number Line

You can use a number line to show the relationships between whole numbers, fractions, or decimals. A number line is a line that has points at regular intervals, and each point has an assigned value. On the TABE you will solve problems using a number line.

Example What decimal goes in the box on the number line?

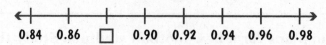

0.84 0.86 ☐ 0.90 0.92 0.94 0.96 0.98

Step 1. First decide on the value of each point along the number line. 0.86 is 0.02 more than 0.84. Add. 0.02 + 0.86 = 0.88

Step 2. To make sure that 0.02 is the correct interval, add 0.02 to 0.88 to see if it will equal the next decimal. 0.88 + 0.02 = 0.90. Each point on the number line is 0.02 more than the one to the left of it.

0.88 should go in the box on the number line.

Test Example

Read the question. Circle the answer.

1   What decimal goes in the box on the number line?

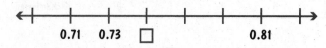

0.71 0.73 ☐ 0.81

A   0.77

B   0.75

C   0.74

D   0.80

1   B Each point on the number line is 0.02 more than the one to the left of it. 0.73 + 0.02 = 0.75.

Hint

Don't forget to line up the decimal points when adding decimals.

Applied Math

Practice

Read the question. Circle the answer.

1 What decimal goes in the box on the number line?

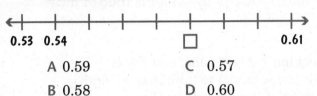

| A 0.59 | C 0.57 |
| B 0.58 | D 0.60 |

2 What decimal goes in the box on the number line?

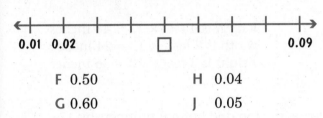

| F 0.50 | H 0.04 |
| G 0.60 | J 0.05 |

3 What decimal goes in the box on the number line?

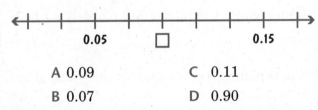

| A 0.09 | C 0.11 |
| B 0.07 | D 0.90 |

4 What decimal goes in the box on the number line?

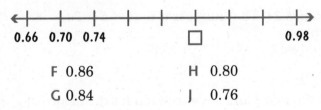

| F 0.86 | H 0.80 |
| G 0.84 | J 0.76 |

5 What decimal goes in the box on the number line?

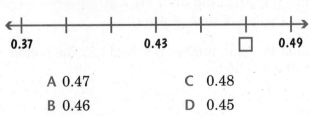

| A 0.47 | C 0.48 |
| B 0.46 | D 0.45 |

6 What decimal goes in the box on the number line?

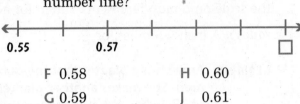

| F 0.58 | H 0.60 |
| G 0.59 | J 0.61 |

7 Steve recorded daily snowfall totals for the past five days on this chart.

Weekly Snowfall

Day	Total Snowfall for week
Monday	0.02 inches
Tuesday	0.03 inches
Wednesday	0.06 inches
Thursday	0.08 inches
Friday	0.10 inches

He wanted to use a number line to plot the amount and the day. Which day would be at 0.06?

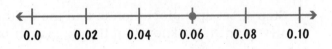

| A Monday | C Thursday |
| B Wednesday | D Tuesday |

8 What decimal goes in the box on the number line?

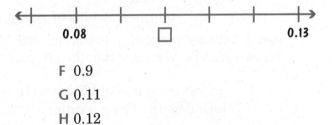

F 0.9

G 0.11

H 0.12

J 0.10

Check your answers on page 122.

Lesson 6 | Ratio and Proportion

You come in contact with ratios every day. Whenever you see the words "nine out of ten," or "miles to the gallon," or "1 inch = 5 miles," you are reading a ratio.

A ratio is a comparison of two numbers, and it can be written as a fraction. For example, if the scale on a map represents 1 inch for every 5 miles, you can say that the ratio of inches to miles is 1 inch = 5 miles, or $\frac{1}{5}$.

Example Angie has a planter that measures 4 feet long, 2 feet wide, and 3 feet high. She makes another planter that is proportional to it but has a length of 12 inches. What is the width and height of the new planter?

Step 1. Determine the scale Angie used to create the second planter. Because the new planter will be in inches, convert all measurements of the old planter to inches. There are 12 inches in a foot, so multiply the number of feet by 12 to get the number of inches.

Step 2. Set up a ratio of the old length and the new one as a fraction: $\frac{48}{12}$

length is **4** feet × **12** = 48 inches
width is **2** feet × **12** = 24 inches
height is **3** feet × **12** = 36 inches

Step 3. Reduce the fraction to its lowest terms. Divide the top and bottom numbers by 12.

$$\frac{48}{12} \div \frac{12}{12} = \frac{4}{1}$$

The ratio of the old planter length to the new planter length is 4 inches (old planter) = 1 inch (new planter), $\frac{4}{1}$.

Step 4. Set up a proportion to find the width of the new planter. Let w stand for the width of the new planter. We know that the old planter is 24 inches wide.

$$\frac{4 \text{ inches (length of \textbf{old planter})}}{1 \text{ inch (length of \textbf{new planter})}} = \frac{24 \text{ inches (width of \textbf{old planter})}}{w \text{ inches (width of \textbf{new planter})}}$$

Now find out what number multiplied by 4 equals 24. That number is 6. (4 × 6 = 24.) Multiply 1 inch × 6 to get the width of the new planter.

$$\frac{4}{1} \times \frac{6}{6} = \frac{24 \text{ inches}}{6 \text{ inches}} \text{ (\textbf{width of new planter})}$$

Step 5. Set up a proportion to find the height of the new planter. Let h stand for the height of the new planter. We know that the old planter is 36 inches high.

$$\frac{4 \text{ inches (length of \textbf{old planter})}}{1 \text{ inch (length of \textbf{new planter})}} = \frac{36 \text{ inches (height of \textbf{old planter})}}{h \text{ inches (height of \textbf{new planter})}}$$

Now find out what number multiplied by 4 equals 36. That number is 9. Multiply the bottom number by 9 to get the height of the new planter. (9 × 4 = 36.)

$$\frac{4}{1} \times \frac{9}{9} = \frac{36 \text{ inches}}{9 \text{ inches}} \text{ (\textbf{height of new planter})}$$

The width of the new planter is 6 inches and the height is 9 inches.

Read the question. Circle the answer.

1 Carmen is building a shed. The blueprints show that a 3-inch line represents a 12-foot side. What scale was used to draw the blueprint?

A   3 inches = 10 feet

B   3 inches = $\frac{1}{2}$ foot

C   1 inch = 4 feet

D   1 inch = 3 feet

Hint

For a proportion, the terms in both ratios have to be kept in the same order. Be sure that you are comparing inches to inches and feet to feet.

1   C   The ratio 3 inches = 12 feet can be written as $\frac{3}{12}$. It can be reduced by dividing each number by 3.

$$\frac{3 \text{ inches}}{12 \text{ feet}} \div \frac{3}{3} = \frac{1 \text{ inch}}{4 \text{ feet}}$$

Practice

Sarah wants to build a new back patio. This diagram shows the dimensions of the patio. Study the diagram. Then answer numbers 1 and 2.

1   A 2-inch line in the diagram represents 6 feet of the patio. What scale is used to draw the diagram?

A 1 inch = 6 feet

B 1 inch = 3 feet

C 1 inch = 2 feet

D I inch = 8 feet

2   Sarah's neighbor Stan wants a new patio for his yard like Sarah's. His patio will have a length of 22 feet. What will be the width of the larger patio?

F   6 feet

G   4 feet

H 15 feet

J 20 feet

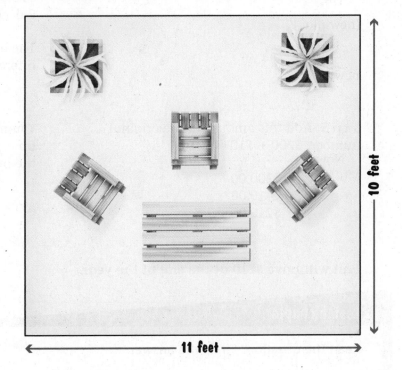

10 feet

11 feet

Check your answers on page 122.

Lesson 7 · Percent

You come in contact with percents every day. Sales tax, inflation rates, and discounts are a few examples. Percents can be written as a fraction. The denominators of these fractions are always 100 because percent means "out of a hundred" parts. Knowing how to use percents can be helpful in solving many types of problems both in everyday life and on the TABE.

Example Phil put $200 in the bank, where it will pay 5% interest per year. How much money will he have at the bank after one year?

Step 1. Change the percent to a decimal. First drop the "%" sign. There's no decimal point, so put one at the right of the number 5. Then move the decimal point two places to the left.

$$5\% \longrightarrow 5. \longrightarrow .05$$

Step 2. Multiply the numbers as if they were both whole numbers.

$$\begin{array}{r} 200 \\ \times\ \ 5 \\ \hline 1{,}000 \end{array}$$

Step 3. Count the places to the right of the decimal point in each number.

$$\begin{array}{ll} 200. \longrightarrow & \textbf{0}\ \text{decimal places} \\ 0.05 \longrightarrow & \underline{+\ \textbf{2}\ \text{decimal places}} \\ & \textbf{2}\ \text{decimal places} \end{array}$$

Step 4. Add the number of decimal places to find the total number of decimal places. Starting at the right of the answer, count to the left the total number of decimal places. Then place the decimal point.

$$1{,}000 \longrightarrow 10.00$$

$10.00
2 decimal places

The amount of interest paid is $10.00.

Hint

Sometimes you'll need to fill places with zeros when placing the decimal in a multiplication problem.

Step 5. Add this amount to the original number: $200 + $10 = $210.

$$\begin{array}{r} \$200.00 \\ +\ \$\ 10.00 \\ \hline \$210.00 \end{array}$$

You may also write 5% as a fraction and set up a proportion. Then add that number to the original number.

$$5\% = \frac{5}{100} = \frac{\$}{200} \longrightarrow \frac{5}{100} \times \frac{2}{2} = \frac{10}{200}$$

Phil will have $210 at the end of the year.

Test Example

Read the question. Circle the answer.

1 Full-grown Indian elephants can be 10 feet tall. African elephants are about 30% taller. About how tall is an African elephant?

    A 16 feet   C 15 feet

    B 11 feet   D 13 feet

1 **D** Change 30% to 0.30 and multiply this by the size of the Indian elephant: 10 feet × 0.30 = 3 feet. To find the size of the African elephant, add 10 feet + 3 feet = 13 feet.

Practice

Read the question. Circle the answer.

1 A CD player sells for $95.99. The sales tax is 7%. What is the total cost for 2 CD players?

A $205.42

B $204.36

C $215.63

D $102.71

2 Emanuel pays 5% of his monthly salary of $2,495.55 to his health-care plan. To compute this payment, he must multiply $2,495.55 by

F 0.005

G 0.5

H 0.05

J 0.0005

3 A snow-removal service offered a one-time special of 20% off their regular fee of $30 per hour. What was the snow removal fee for 103 hours of work?

A $2,090.00

B $2,472.00

C $2,137.00

D $2,060.00

Study this advertisement for a sale. Then do numbers 4 and 5.

4 There is a 6% sales tax. If you pay cash, what is the total cost of the blouse with tax?

F $53.00   H $54.00

G $52.00   J $56.00

5 If you buy the blouse through the installment plan, what is the amount of the down payment?

A $1.06   C $10.00

B $5.30   D $10.60

Check your answers on pages 122–123.

Operation Properties

For the operations of addition and multiplication, reversing the order of two numbers does not change the result. For example, $4 + 5 = 9$ and $5 + 4 = 9$. This is called the *Commutative Property*.

In addition and multiplication, moving parentheses or brackets will not change the result. For example, $2 \times (5 \times 3) = 30$ and $(2 \times 5) \times 3 = 30$. This is called the *Associative Property*.

A special property applies to expressions where the sum of two numbers is multiplied by a third number, such as $6 \times (3 + 4)$. This property is called the *Distributive Property*. It means that $6 \times (3 + 4)$ is the same as $(6 \times 3) + (6 \times 4)$. Both expressions equal 42.

These properties can make it easier to solve certain types of problems.

Example **You are asked to solve the problem $(4 \times 97) + (4 \times 3) = ?$**

Step 1. Use the *Distributive Property* to simplify the problem.

$$4 \times (97 + 3) = ?$$

Step 2. Add $97 + 3$ to get 100.

$$4 \times 100 = ?$$

Step 3. Multiply 4 by 100 to get 400.

$$4 \times 100 = 400$$

$$(4 \times 97) + (4 \times 3) = 400$$

Test Example

Read the question. Circle the answer.

1   Which of the following expressions is equal to 12×6 using the *Commutative Property*?

    A 16×2

    B 21×6

    C 6×12

    D 2×16

Hint

Use the *Distributive Property* to simplify multiplication problems. The problem 7×102 can become $(7 \times 100) + (7 \times 2)$.

1 **C** 6×12 Since 6×12 will give you the same result as 12×6, this is an example of the *Commutative Property*.

Read the questions. Circle the answer.

1 Which of the following equations is an example of the *Associative Property*?

A $8 + (4 \times 5) = (8 \times 4) + (8 \times 5)$

B $20 + 6 = 6 + 20$

C $(3 + 5) + 9 = 3 \times (5 + 9)$

D $7 + (8 + 2) = (7 + 8) + 2$

2 Which of the following expressions is equal to $(3 + 6) \times 7$ using the *Distributive Property*?

F $7 \times (3 + 6)$

G $3 + (6 \times 7)$

H $(3 \times 7) + (6 \times 7)$

J $(3 \times 7) + (3 \times 6)$

3 Which of the following pairs of expressions are equal using the *Commutative Property*?

A $5 + 13$ and $13 + 5$

B $26 - 8$ and $8 - 26$

C 4×10 and 40×0

D $9 \div 3$ and $3 \div 9$

4 Which of the following pairs of expressions are equal using the *Associative Property*?

F $3 \times (7 \times 4)$ and $(3 \times 7) + 4$

G $(10 \times 6) \times 11$ and $10 \times (6 \times 11)$

H $4 \times (3 \times 5)$ and $4 + (3 \times 5)$

J $(6 \times 9) \times 2$ and $6 + 9 \times 2$

5 Which of the following expressions is equal to $(81 \times 9) + (81 \times 1)$ using the *Distributive Property*?

A $81 \times (9 + 1)$

B $(81 \times 1) \times (81 \times 9)$

C $(81 \times 9) + 1$

D $(81 + 1) \times 9$

6 Which of the following equations is an example of the *Commutative Property*?

F $6 \times 5 = 5 + 6$

G $13 - 3 = 10 + 3$

H $20 \div 5 = 5 \div 20$

J $9 + 35 = 35 + 9$

7 Which of the following equations is an example of the *Distributive Property*?

A $13 \times (4 + 5) = 13 \times 4 + 5$

B $17 + (2 \times 6) = (17 \times 2) + (17 \times 6)$

C $21 \times (9 + 11) = (21 \times 9) + (11 \times 9)$

D $(15 + 5) \times 3 = (15 \times 3) + (5 \times 3)$

8 Which of the following properties is illustrated by the equation $3 \times (5 \times 4) = (3 \times 5) \times 4$?

F Commutative Property

G Associative Property

H Distributive Property

J none of the above

Check your answers on page 123.

Lesson 9 Factors, Multiples, and Divisibility

Numbers that can be multiplied together to get a product are called factors of that product. For example, 5 and 7 are factors of 35 since $5 \times 7 = 35$. The number 35 is a multiple of 5, and a multiple of 7. Both 5 and 7 can be multiplied by a number to get 35. When 35 is divided by 5 or 7, the quotient is a whole number. This means that the number 35 is divisible by 5 and 7.

Example What are the factors of 30?

Step 1. Think of a number that can divide evenly into 30. Because 30 is an even number, it can be divided by 2.

$$30 \div 2 = 15.$$

Step 2. Think of a number that can divide evenly into 15. The number 5 is one example since $15 \div 5 = 3$.

Step 3. List the factors 2, 3, and 5. They are prime numbers since they do not have any other factors except themselves and 1. Check whether 2×3, 2×5, and 3×5 divide evenly into 30.

Step 4. List all the factors of 30 including 1 and 30: 1, 2, 3, 5, 6, 10, 15, and 30.

The factors of 30 are 1, 2, 3, 5, 6, 10, 15, and 30.

Test Example

Read the question. Circle the answer.

1 Which number is a multiple of 6?

   A 9

   B 16

   C 24

   D 35

Hint

Numbers are always a multiple of 3 if their digits add up to a multiple of 3. Try the number 69. $6 + 9 = 15$, which is a multiple of 3. So 69 is a multiple of 3.

1 **C** Because $6 \times 4 = 24$, 24 is a multiple of 6.

Read the questions. Circle the answer.

1 Which list of numbers shows all the factors of 12?

A 2, 3, 4, 6

B 1, 2, 3, 4, 5, 6, 12

C 1, 3, 4, 12

D 1, 2, 3, 4, 6, 12

2 Which number is divisible by 4?

F 54

G 34

H 32

J 18

3 Which number is a multiple of 12?

A 35

B 3

C 72

D 102

4 Which number is a factor of 21?

F 7

G 12

H 2

J 63

5 Which list of numbers shows all the factors of 45?

A 1, 3, 5, 9, 15, 30, 45

B 1, 3, 5, 9, 15, 45

C 1, 3, 4, 5, 9, 15, 30, 45

D 1, 3, 9, 15, 30, 45

6 Which number is a multiple of 15?

F 5

G 25

H 115

J 90

7 Which number is a factor of 25?

A 100

B 7

C 50

D 5

8 Which number is divisible by 3?

F 141

G 152

H 124

J 182

Check your answers on page 123.

Solve. Circle the answer.

1 What is another way to write 2.6?

A $\dfrac{6}{10}$

B $2\dfrac{3}{5}$

C Two and six-hundredths

D $2\dfrac{6}{100}$

2 Kevin adds a 10% tip to his bill at the restaurant. To compute this tip, he should multiply $14.50 by

F 0.10   **H** 0.0001

G 0.01   **J** 1.00

The United States measures about 3,000 miles from east to west and 2,000 miles from north to south. Karen wants to draw a map of the United States.

3 Two inches on the map represents 600 miles. What scale was used to draw the map?

A 2 inches = 3,000 miles

B 2 inches = 300 miles

C 1 inch = 300 miles

D 1 inch = 600 miles

4 Karen plans to draw a map of one section of the country that is proportional to the actual section. If the actual distance from north to south of this section is 1,000 miles, what is the actual distance of the section from east to west?

F 2,000 miles

G 1,500 miles

H 2,500 miles

J 1,000 miles

5 If 0.25 of people chose pizza as their favorite lunch, what fraction of people chose pizza?

A $\dfrac{1}{3}$ **C** $\dfrac{1}{2}$

B $\dfrac{2}{5}$ **D** $\dfrac{1}{4}$

6 In Canada about 14 people live on every 2 square miles of land. About how many people would live on 10 square miles of land?

F 80

G 60

H 70

J 50

7 The chart below shows some people's weight gain last week.

Weight Gain

Name	Weight Gain Pounds
Sylvia	0.30
Mel	0.75
Etta	$\dfrac{6}{20}$
Herm	$\dfrac{20}{100}$

Who gained the same amount of weight last week?

A Sylvia and Etta

B Mel and Etta

C Herm and Sylvia

D Herm and Mel

8 A 3-inch line on a diagram of a backyard represents 12 feet. What scale was used to draw the diagram of the backyard?

F 1 inch = 3 feet

G 1 inch = 5 feet

H 1 inch = 4 feet

J 1 inch = 2 feet

9 Chocolate candies sell for $5.60 a dozen. Sales tax is 7%. What is the total cost for 2 dozen candies?

A $0.78

B $11.98

C $5.99

D $12.95

10 Adult polar bears may weigh as much as 1,600 pounds. In a year when food is scarce, they may weigh 20% less than normal. If food is scarce, how much would be the combined weight of 5 polar bears?

F 7,200 pounds

G 8,000 pounds

H 6,400 pounds

J 5,200 pounds

11 Which percent is equal to 3/4?

A 75%

B 15%

C 25%

D 50%

12 A basketball team won 60 of its 80 games. What percentage of its games did the team lose?

F 50%

G 25%

H 20%

J 60%

13 Which property is illustrated by the equation below?

$5 \times (4 \times 10) = (5 \times 4) \times 10$

A Associative Property

B Commutative Property

C Distributive Property

D none of the above

14 Which list shows all the factors of 30?

F 1, 2, 3, 5, 6, and 30

G 1, 2, 3, 4, 5, 6, 8, 10, 12, 15, and 30

H 1, 2, 3, 5, 6, 10, 15, and 30

J 1, 2, 3, 5, 6, 10, 12, 15, 20, and 30

Check your answers on pages 123.

Lesson 10 Graphs

You see graphs in newspapers or magazines every day. Graphs give the reader a quick understanding of a set of numbers.

Example **On which two days were the dollar amounts of sales the same?**

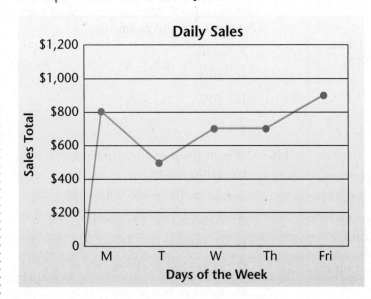

Step 1. Look at the graph. The left-hand side of the graph (total sales in dollars) is called the vertical axis because it starts at the bottom corner and points up. The bottom of the graph (days of the week) is called the horizontal axis because it starts at the bottom corner and points across to the right.

Step 2. Because you are looking for two days on which sales were the same, look for two points of the same height. Check along the vertical axis to make sure the sales totals are the same. Look along the horizontal axis to find the days on which sales were the same.

Sales were the same on Wednesday and Thursday.

Test Example

Read the question. Circle the answer.

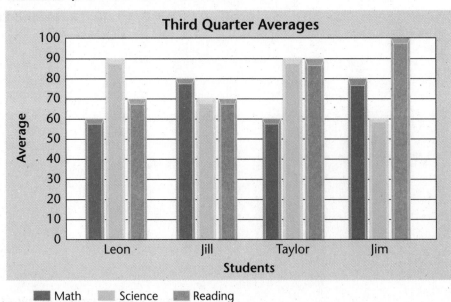

1   Which student had the smallest difference between his or her best and worst average?

A   Jim

B   Leon

C   Taylor

D   Jill

1 · **D** There was a difference of 10 points in Jill's best and worst subjects. Leon and Taylor each had a 30-point difference, and there was a 40-point difference for Jim.

Practice

Read the question. Circle the answer.

This graph shows men's and women's college sports participation from 1991 through 1994. Study the graph. Then do numbers 1 and 2.

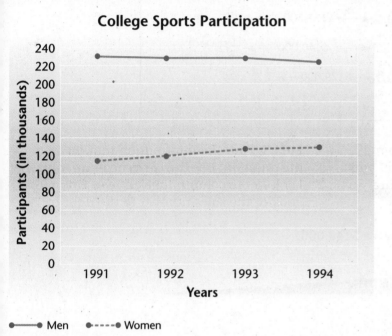

College Sports Participation

●——● Men   ●----● Women

1 In what period will you find the greatest difference in the participation of men and women?

A 1992

B 1991

C 1994

D 1993

2 During what period had women's participation increased the most from the previous period?

F 1994

G 1992

H 1991

J 1993

This graph shows the percentage of income spent on different categories of expenses by different age groups. Study the graph. Then do numbers 3 and 4.

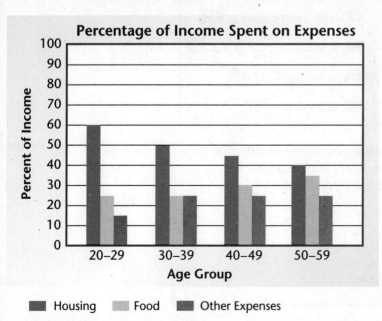

Percentage of Income Spent on Expenses

■ Housing   ▨ Food   ■ Other Expenses

3 Which age group uses the largest percentage of its income for housing?

A 50–59

B 40–49

C 20–29

D 30–39

4 Which age group spends approximately half as much for food as it does for housing?

F 30–39   H 50–59

G 20–29   J 40–49

Check your answers on page 123.

Lesson 11 Charts

William made a chart to show the annual sales of his company. The chart made it easy for his staff to read and compare the sales. Learning how to read charts can help you solve many types of problems on the TABE.

Example The chart below show the annual sales of William's popcorn company. What were his company's sales in 1990?

Yearly Sales

Year	Sales
1985	← $137,000 →
1990	← $140,000 →
1995	← $129,000 →
2000	← $1,000,000 →

Step 1. Read the question carefully to make sure you understand what information you are looking for. In this example you are looking for the **sales** in **1990**.

Step 2. Find the information that answers the question. Use the correct column and row. Look in the column labeled *Year*. Find 1990. Look at the sales number to the right of 1990.

The sales of this company in 1990 were $140,000.

Test Example

Read the question. Circle the answer.

Number of Trees

Tree Type	How Many
Sugar Maple	← 15 →
Sycamore	← 17 →
Black Oak	← 10 →
Basswood	← 8 →

1 Hank, a park ranger, made a chart to show the number of types of trees in one section of the park. How many sycamore trees are in this part of the park?

A 10

B 15

C 17

D 8

1 C This section of the park has 17 sycamore trees.

Read the question. Circle the answer.

This chart shows the grams of fiber in a 1-cup serving of several types of grains. Study the chart. Then do number 1.

Fiber Content in 1-Cup Serving

Food	Grams of Fiber
Brown Rice	←6.5→
Bulgur Wheat	←25.6→
Barley	←31.8→
Millet	←17.0→

1 What is the fiber content in one cup of bulgur wheat?

A 6.5 grams   C 31.8 grams

B 25.6 grams   D 17.0 grams

The chart shows the number of restaurants in certain towns in Kansas. Study the chart. Then do numbers 2 and 3.

Kansas Restaurants

Town	How Many
Smithville	←68→
Clarksdale	←97→
Milltown	←35→
Sanderson	←80→
Trenttown	←75→

2 Which town has the most restaurants?

F Milltown   H Smithville

G Sanderson   J Clarksdale

3 What is the best estimate of the average number of restaurants?

A 80   C 70

B 90   D 60

Jackie made a chart to show the number of points scored by some hockey teams. Study the chart. Then do numbers 4 through 6.

Hockey Points

Team	Points
Ottawa	←80→
Nashville	←70→
Minnesota	←90→
Phoenix	←35→
Carolina	←50→

4 How many points has Nashville scored?

F 80

G 60

H 70

J 50

5 How many total points have the top two teams scored?

A 120 points

B 165 points

C 115 points

D 170 points

6 Which statement about the chart is true?

F Ottawa had a much better season last year.

G Phoenix will score 65 more points this season.

H Nashville must score 20 more points to catch Ottawa.

J Minnesota is 20 points ahead of Nashville.

Check your answers on page 123.

Data recorded on a graph, in a chart, or on a table can be used to show whether some statements are true or false. When data shows that a statement is true, that statement is known as a *conclusion from the data*.

Example **This table shows the number of hits that each player on Hector's baseball team had this season.**

13	21	15	2	4	8	16	11	5	18	6	10

State a conclusion that can be drawn from the data.

Step 1. Find out what the data describes. This table shows the number of hits each player on Hector's baseball team had this season.

Step 2. Organize the data in the most convenient way possible. In this case, arrange the numbers from least to greatest.

2	4	5	6	8	10	11	13	15	16	18	21

Step 3. Decide what statements can be drawn from the data.

Most of the players on Hector's baseball team have 10 or more hits this season.

Step 4. Check to be sure the statement is true.

There are 5 players on the team with fewer than 10 hits, and 7 players with 10 or more hits. Most of the players have 10 or more hits.

Test Example

Read the question. Circle the answer.

1 Sam asked 50 students at his school to name their favorite band. What conclusions might he be able to draw from his survey?

    A which band is most popular across the United States

    B how much time his classmates spend listening to music

    C which band is most popular at his school

    D whether his classmates have good taste in music

Hint

A conclusion cannot be drawn from data unless the conclusion matches the information in the data.

1 **C** His survey gives data about which band is the favorite among his classmates. It does not give data on the other questions.

Read the questions. Circle the answer.

This table shows information about the solar system. Study the table. Then complete questions 1 through 3.

Name	Mass (in relation to Earth)	Distance from Sun (in AU)
Mercury	0.4	0.06
Venus	0.7	0.8
Earth	1	1
Mars	0.1	1.5
Jupiter	318	5.2
Saturn	95	9.5
Neptune	14	19.2
Uranus	17	30.0

1 Which conclusion can the data support?

A Three planets in the solar system have less mass than Earth.

B Earth is the only planet on which people can live.

C Some planets in the solar system are more than 500 AUs from the sun.

D All planets must be at least one-third the mass of Earth.

2 Which subject can the data support?

F the mass and distance of planets orbiting other stars

G the distance between the sun and the nearest star

H the cost of sending space craft to other planets in the solar system

J the distance from the sun of planets in the solar system

3 Which conclusion can be made about Earth from the data?

A Earth has neither the largest nor smallest mass.

B The distance of the Earth from the sun is the greatest among the planets.

C Earth has neither the largest nor smallest surface area.

D The Earth has more mass and is farther from the sun than Mars.

This table shows information about Alex's grades in Science and History. Study the table and then do questions 4 through 6.

Month	Science Grade	History Grade
September	80	92
October	82	91
November	85	89
December	87	88
January	89	86
February	90	85
March	93	82
April	94	81

4 Which conclusion can the data support?

F Alex studied hard and did all of his homework.

G Alex's science grades increased.

H Alex should have studied history more.

J Alex's history grades are always better than his science grades.

5 Which subject can the data support?

A Alex's English grades

B the grades Alex's sister gets in science and history

C the difficulty of the science and history textbooks

D changes in Alex's grades in science and history

6 Which conclusion can be made about Alex's grades from September to April?

F His overall grades improved.

G His science grades improved and his history grades got worse.

H His science grades got worse and his history grades improved.

J His overall grades improved until December and then got worse.

Check your answers on page 124.

Appropriate Data Display

Data is easier to understand when it is shown in the appropriate type of display. Changes over time are most appropriately displayed on line graphs. Percentages are best shown on circle graphs. Quantities are compared using bar graphs. Using the appropriate graph to display data is an important part of reporting information.

Example **Ralph attends a two-hour recreational class every Monday. During the class, he spends a half hour painting, one hour playing tennis, and a half hour playing on a computer. What type of graph is the best choice to display the percentage of time Ralph spends on each activity?**

Because the data displayed shows percentages of the total time that Ralph spends at the recreational class, the data is best displayed in a circle graph.

Test Example

Read the question. Circle the answer.

1 Carmen recorded these temperatures outside her school on September 6.

Time	9 a.m.	11 a.m.	1 p.m.	3 p.m.
Temperature	4°C	6°C	2°C	1°C

Which type of display is most appropriate for showing Carmen's data?

A   a line graph

B   a circle graph

C   a bar graph

D   none of the above

Hint

The sections on a circle graph show how something is divided between various parts. The line on a line graph shows something increasing or decreasing over time.

1 **A** Because the data shows the change in temperature over time, the data is best displayed on a line graph.

Read the questions. Circle the answer.

1 Which data would be most appropriately displayed on a bar graph?

A the population of different states in 2008

B the depth of snow as it falls throughout the day

C the percentage of visitors to a museum from different age groups

D the changes in someone's bank account as they add and withdraw money

2 Which data would be best displayed on a circle graph?

F the number of answers wrong by 12 students on the same test

G the change of water level in a bath tub throughout a day

H the percentage of voters who vote for different candidates

J the temperature of a classroom throughout the day

3 Which data would be most appropriately shown on a line graph?

A the number of miles walked by 10 different volunteers at a charity walk-a-thon

B the percentage of customers ordering each selection on a menu

C the land area of different countries

D the changing height of an airplane during its flight

4 Elissa has recorded how much time she spends doing homework for each of her classes. Which type of display would be most appropriate for recording the percentage of time she spends doing homework for each class?

F a line graph

G a circle graph

H a bar graph

J none of the above

5 Which data would not be most appropriately displayed on a bar graph?

A the number of birds counted in ten different towns

B the number of miles on different plane flights

C the growth of a bean plant over 5 weeks

D the number of cans donated by different classes in a school's food drive

6 Which data would not be best displayed on a line graph?

F the change in a train's speed as it travels from one city to another

G the percentages of people who prefer different radio stations

H the change in the unemployment rate in a city over a year

J the change in water level at a reservoir

7 Which data would not be most appropriately shown on a circle graph?

A the percentage of people choosing various favorite sports

B the percentage of different flavors purchased in ice cream sales

C the percentage of a school day that Nora studies various subjects

D the height of a rocket at different times after blast-off

8 Ichiro is preparing a display that will compare the weights of his four pets. Which type of display would be most appropriate for recording his pets' weights?

F a line graph

G a circle graph

H a bar graph

J none of the above

Check your answers on page 124.

Solve. Circle the answer.

1 Mrs. Harris wants to make a graph showing the number of books read by each student in her class. Which type of graph would be most appropriate?

    A bar graph

    B line graph

    C circle graph

    D none of the above

2 Mrs. Harris also wants to make a graph that shows the total number of books read by her class each month. Which type of graph would be most appropriate?

    F bar graph

    G line graph

    H circle graph

    J none of the above

This graph shows the operating expenses for Mark's business over the last 5 years. Study the graph. Then do numbers 3 through 6.

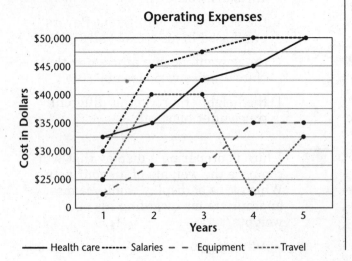

Operating Expenses

3 If the expenses continue to increase as they did during the fourth year, which expense can Mark expect to increase the most from the fifth to sixth year?

    A travel

    B health care

    C equipment

    D salaries

4 Which of these is the best estimate for the total operating costs for the second year?

    F $35,000

    G $64,500

    H $150,000

    J $37,500

5 In year 4, expenses from least to greatest are

    A salaries, equipment, health care, travel

    B travel, equipment, health care, salaries

    C salaries, health care, equipment, travel

    D health care, health care, travel

6 Which expense is less in the fourth year than it was in the second year?

    F health care

    G travel

    H salaries

    J equipment

7 Wayne is studying a line graph that shows the elevation of an airplane as it flies from San Francisco to Chicago. Which of the following could he conclude from the line graph?

A the number of passengers on the airplane

B the speed of the airplane

C the maximum altitude reached by the airplane

D the size of the airplane

8 The chart shows the money collected during a 7-hour book sale. Which of these is the best estimate of the average amount of money collected each hour?

Money Collected

Hour	Amount
1	$287
2	$219
3	$325
4	$197
5	$268
6	$250
7	$149

F $240   H $230

G $260   J $280

9 The price of a television is $400. When the 4% sales tax is added to this price, what is the total cost of the television?

A $420

B $416

C $412

D $425

10 Kim is making a graph to show the change in temperature throughout the day. Which type of graph would be most appropriate?

F bar graph

G line graph

H circle graph

J none of the above

This chart shows some of Canada's imports. Study the chart. Then do numbers 11 and 12.

Canada's Imports

Product	Percent of Total Imports
Autos and Parts	30%
Machinery and Equipment	27%
Mining Products	7%

11 Which of these statements is supported by the information in the table?

A Mining products make up the smallest percentage of imports shown on the graph.

B Mining products make up $\frac{1}{3}$ of all of Canada's imports.

C Autos and Parts make up the smallest percentage of Canada's imports.

D Machinery and Equipment is the most important import of Canada.

12 What percentage of Canada's imports is represented in this chart?

F 62%   H 58%

G 64%   J 39%

Check your answers on page 124.

Lesson 14 Probability and Statistics

An average is a number that best represents all the numbers in a group. You probably come in contact with averages every day: a bowling average or the average income for a particular job. A median is a type of average. It is the number that falls exactly in the middle of a set of numbers when the numbers are arranged in order of least to greatest.

Example The weekly earnings of five people are shown in the chart. What is the best estimate of their average weekly earnings? What is the best estimate of the median earnings?

Earnings

Carlos	$759
Loretta	$197
Andy	$553
Marcia	$905
Darryl	$431

Step 1. Find the average. First add the numbers in the list. Regroup as needed.

$$
\begin{array}{r}
^{22}\ \\
\$759 \\
\$197 \\
\$553 \\
\$905 \\
+\ \$431 \\
\hline
\$2,845
\end{array}
$$

Step 2. Next count the numbers in the list and divide the sum by that amount. There are 5 numbers in the list, so divide $2,845 by 5. $569 is the average weekly income.

$$
\begin{array}{r}
569 \\
5\ )\overline{2845} \\
-25 \\
\hline
34 \\
-30 \\
\hline
45 \\
-45 \\
\end{array}
$$

Step 3. Because the question asks for the best "estimate," round the answer to the nearest ten.

$569

9 is greater than 5, so add 1 to the 6 in the tens place and change the 9 in the ones place to 0. $569 is rounded up to $570.

Step 4. To find the median, arrange the numbers from least to greatest. The number in the middle is known as the median. Because the problem asks for the best estimate, round the median to the nearest ten.

$197 $431 $553 $759 $905

3 is less than 5, so the 5 in the tens place remains unchanged. Change the 3 in the tens place to 0. $553 is rounded down to $550.

The average weekly earnings estimate is $570. The median weekly earnings estimate is $550.

Study the chart. Circle the answer.

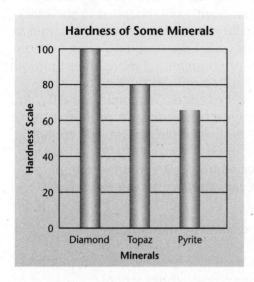

Hardness of Some Minerals

1 What is the best estimate of the average hardness of these minerals?

A 80

B 70

C 100

D 10,060

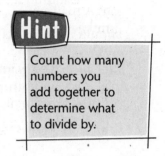

Hint

Count how many numbers you add together to determine what to divide by.

1 **A** Add 100 + 80 + 63 = 243. You have 3 minerals, so you will divide by 3. 243 ÷ 3 = 81. 81 rounded down to the nearest ten is 80.

Practice

This graph shows the countries supplying the most oil to the United States. Study the graph. Then do number 1.

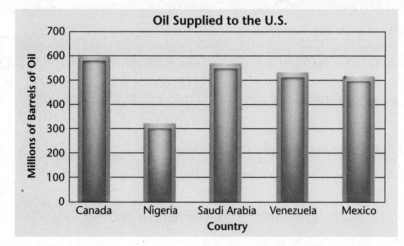

Oil Supplied to the U.S.

1 Which of these is the best estimate of the median amount of oil supplied by the five countries?

A 300 million barrels

B 400 million barrels

C 600 million barrels

D 500 million barrels

Check your answers on page 124.

Lesson 15 • Sampling

A sample is a selected group of people or things used when it is not possible to study every person or thing in a population. For instance, it is not possible to survey every person in the United States. Instead, a survey may obtain information from 1,000 people and use that information to represent everyone in the country. The difference between data obtained from a sample and data that is true of the whole population is called the sampling error. When a sample is chosen so that some parts of the population are represented more often than others, the sample is biased. The results of a survey with a biased sample will not be accurate.

In designing a survey or other research, it is important to choose a sample correctly. An incorrect sample will lead to inaccurate data and improper conclusions. A random sample should lead to accurate data and conclusions as long as the sample size is large enough.

Example **Lee wants to know how every student at her school feels about the school uniforms. She doesn't have time to talk to every student, so she will select a sample.**

How should Lee select a random sample of students at her school?

Step 1. Lee should decide how many students she has time to interview. Lee can talk to 15 students a day, so she can interview 75 students over 5 days at her school.

Step 2. Lee should find one or more locations where all the students in the school are equally likely to go. Lee decides to conduct her survey in the hallway nearest the restrooms.

Step 3. Lee should conduct interviews at the chosen location at times when she is most likely to speak to the broadest range of students. Because some students only attend school in the morning and some students only attend in the afternoon, Lee will conduct her survey from 8 to 9 a.m. and from 2 to 3 p.m.

Test Example

Read the question. Circle the answer.

1 Imani wants to determine the weight of the hailstones that fell in today's hailstorm in her town. Which choice will give her a random sample of hailstones?

   A 10 friends each brings in the largest hailstones they find

   B 1,000 hailstones found near Imani's house

   C 100 hailstones picked up at random in locations all over town

   D 250 hailstones that are able to pass through a strainer

Hint

A random sample should reflect the larger population as much as possible. It should not be chosen for any special characteristics.

1 **C** Answers A and D are biased because certain types of hailstones are chosen. Answer B only reflects the hailstones near Imani's house, not all the hailstones that fell in her town.

Read the questions. Circle the answer.

1 Which sample is <u>not</u> a random sample?

  A 100 people interviewed in a large parking lot

  B 10,000 people who respond to a survey on an internet site

  C 2,000 telephone numbers selected from a phone directory

  D 1,000 boxes selected from a manufacturing plant

2 Which type of sample would *best* reflect the people who are voting in a town election?

  F 100 people leaving different voting locations

  G 50 people at a gas station

  H 500 people at the rally for one of the candidates

  J 1,000 people in a neighboring state

3 Which sample would *best* represent all the students at a certain school?

  A the winners of the school's scholastic competition

  B the students in detention for not doing their homework

  C the 100 students who have been at the school the least amount of time

  D 50 students chosen at random from a list of all students

4 Which sample is <u>not</u> a random sample?

  F 50 pencils that failed a factory's quality control test

  G 10 computers selected at random from a warehouse

  H 100 apples randomly selected at a processing plant

  J 75 used batteries collected from random houses

5 Which sample would *best* represent the opinions of a store's customers?

  A 100 people leaving the store

  B 150 people shopping at a different store

  C 75 people who are employees of the store

  D 25 phone numbers selected from a city phone directory

6 Which sample of voters would be most likely to have bias?

  F a sample taken at one of the voting locations

  G a sample taken at one of the candidate's rallies

  H a sample taken at random from a city phone book

  J a sample taken in several large parking lots

7 Which sample is a random sample?

  A 50 champion racehorses to represent all horses

  B 100 people who answer a newspaper ad to take a survey

  C 75 snowflakes from 75 different snow storms

  D 100 birds brought to a rescue center to represent all birds

8 Which sample would *best* represent all the employees of a certain company?

  F 75 managers at a business meeting

  G the 20 employees who have been employee of the month

  H 50 employees chosen at random from the payroll list of the company

  J the first 100 employees to arrive at the office on a holiday

Check your answers on page 124.

1 Which sample would *best* represent all the students at a school?

   A 25 members of the honor society

   B 50 members of the football team

   C 75 students randomly chosen from a list of all students

   D 100 students in the school parking lot

2 Which sample would most likely have bias?

   F 25 Olympic athletes to represent all people

   G 50 boxes of cereal from a warehouse

   H 100 voters selected at random from a phone directory

   J 30 people selected at random walking down the streets of a town

3 Which number gives the mean of the populations on the table?

City	Population
Brownville	1,243
East City	2,511
Summer City	734
Old Town	3,192

   A 1,920

   B 7,680

   C 2,191

   D 734

4 Which sample would *best* represent the population of the four cities?

   F 10 people on a street in East City

   G 100 people selected from the phone directories for each city

   H callers to a radio program broadcast to the cities

   J the members of the city councils of the four cities

5 Which number would be a good estimate for the price of Snorgols, according to the table?

Store	Price of Snorgols
Store A	$2.65
Store B	$2.15
Store C	$2.27
Store D	$2.53

A $1.35

B $2.30

C $10.24

D $0.75

6 Which of the following would be the *best* way to get a representative sample of Snorgols being sold at the stores?

F   collecting all Snorgols returned to Customer Service with complaints

G   getting samples from the factory's Quality Control department

H   taking 10 samples at random from each store

J   asking your friends for any Snorgols they have purchased

The tax revenues of a certain state are shown on the table below. Study the graph. Then do 7 and 8.

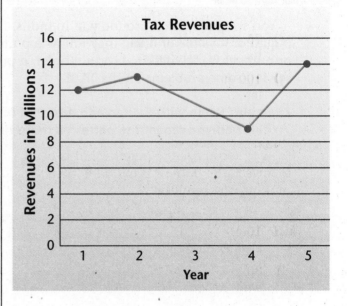

7 Which is a good estimate of the revenues of the state in an average year?

A $8 million   C $16 million

B $11 million   D $19 million

8 George estimates that next year's revenues for the state will be $25 million. How would you evaluate his estimate?

F   This is a good estimate because it is more than year 5.

G   This is a bad estimate because it is very different from the given numbers.

H   This is a good estimate because it is the total of years 4 and 5.

J   This is a bad estimate because revenues go down in even numbered years.

Check your answers on pages 124–125.

Lesson 16 Functions and Patterns

You see patterns all around you in quilts, tile floors, and brick patios. When someone makes a quilt or lays tile or brick, they follow a pattern to get a particular result. When a shape, color, or number is repeated in a certain order, a pattern is created. Recognizing patterns is one way of solving some problems on the TABE.

Example Begin with 5, then add 4 to that number. Next, multiply that answer by 2. If you repeat the pattern 3 more times, what number will you get?

Step 1. Recognize the pattern that is being followed. The pattern is to add 4, then multiply the result by 2.

Step 2. Set up a table using 5 as the starting number. Repeat the pattern 3 more times.

Number	Add 4	Multiply by 2
5	5 + 4 = 9	9 × 2 = 18
18	18 + 4 = 22	22 × 2 = 44
44	44 + 4 = 48	48 × 2 = 96
96	96 + 4 = 100	100 × 2 = 200

If you repeat the pattern three more times, you will get 200.

Test Example

The table shows "Input" numbers that have been changed to "Output" numbers by following a rule. What number is missing from the table?

Rule: Divide by 2, then subtract 2.

Input	Output
64	30
60	28
24	
10	3

Hint

Read the rule carefully before you begin.

A 16   C 12

B 8   D 10

1 D The rule is to divide each "Input" number by 2 and then subtract 2. If the "Input" number is 24, then 24 ÷ 2 = 12; 12 − 2 = 10.

Read the question. Circle the answer.

1 Sarah can seal 6 envelopes in 20 seconds. How many envelopes would you predict she could seal in 60 seconds?

A 20

B 60

C 18

D 24

2 If you start with 2, multiply that number by 3, then keep multiplying the answer you get each time by 3, you will never get which of these numbers?

F 52

G 18

H 162

J 54

3 The table shows "Input" numbers that have been changed by a certain rule to get "Output" numbers. What number is missing from the table?

Input	5	15	25	40	50
Output	1	3	5		10

A 5

B 4

C 9

D 8

4 Sound can travel about 700 meters every 2 seconds. How far can sound travel in 10 seconds?

F 4,000 meters

G 1,750 meters

H 3,500 meters

J 7,000 meters

5 The table shows "Input" numbers that have been changed to "Output" numbers by applying a specific rule. What number is missing from the table?

Rule: Multiply by 4, then subtract 2.

Input	Output
3	10
6	
8	30
9	34

A 22 C 20

B 24 D 26

This graph shows the number of passenger miles traveled, in billions of miles, by automobiles from 1940 to 1980. Study the graph. Then do number 6.

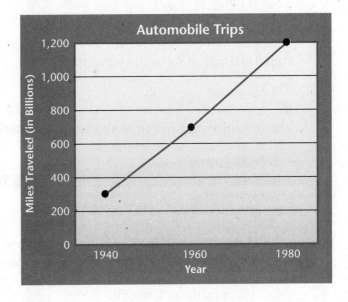

6 If the pattern continues, how many billions of passenger miles would be traveled in 2000?

F 2,200 H 2,000

G 1,800 J 1,700

Check your answers on page 125.

Lesson 17 · Variables, Expressions, and Equations

Expressions are groups of numbers and variables. Equations are number sentences. Expressions and equations may be used to solve problems. In equations, an unknown value is represented by an italic letter, such as *n*. In equations, parentheses are used to show items that go together. Parentheses are also used to show multiplication instead of using the "×" sign: $(n)(750)$ is the same as n times 750, or $750n$. You will be asked to solve equations on the TABE.

Example Over three days, a baby slept 16 hours one day, 17 hours the second day, and 15 hours on the third day. Find the average number of hours the baby slept each day.

Step 1. Choose the letter *x* to represent the answer you must find, which is the unknown.

Step 2. Show the total number of hours the baby slept each day.

$$16 + 17 + 15$$

Step 3. To find an average, you need to divide the sum, or total, by the number of days (3). Use a letter to represent the unknown. Write out the equation that will be used to solve the problem.

$$\frac{(16 + 17 + 15)}{3} = x$$

Step 4. Solve the problem in parentheses first. Add $16 + 17 + 15 = 48$.

$$\frac{48}{3} = x$$

Step 5. Divide to solve the equation.

$$x = 48 \div 3 = 16$$

The average number of hours the baby slept in a day was 16 hours.

Test Example

Read the question. Circle the answer.

1 A movie runs for 94 minutes. There are 5 showings each day. Which equation can be used to show the total time, in hours and minutes, that this movie runs each day? (60 minutes = 1 hour)

A $(94 \div 5) \times 60 = x$

B $(94 \times 60) \div 5 = x$

C $(94 \times 5) \div 60 = x$

D $(94 \times 60) \div 5 = x$

 Hint

How do you change minutes into hours? There are 60 minutes in each hour, so divide the number of minutes by 60.

1 C By multiplying 94×5, you find the total minutes the film is showing each day. By dividing this sum by 60, you change the total minutes into hours and minutes.

Read the question. Circle the answer.

1 Clark can buy 4 pencils for $1.00. He has $5.00 to spend. Clark uses the expression 4×5 to find out how many pencils he can buy. What does this expression represent?

A the number of pencils Clark can buy with $1.00

B the amount of money Clark has

C the amount of money Clark can spend

D the number of pencils Clark can buy

2 In which of these equations is b equal to 20?

F $b + 5 = 25$ 　　　 H $20 - b = 25$

G $b + 25 = 5$ 　　　 J $b - 25 = 20$

Barbara earns $1,889.75 per month. The table below shows the federal and state deductions that are subtracted from her monthly paycheck. Study the table. Then do number 3.

FEDERAL DEDUCTIONS	
Federal Income Tax:	$227.78
Social Security Tax:	$113.89
Medicare Tax:	$27.44

STATE DEDUCTIONS	
State Income Tax:	$34.83
State Unemployment Insurance and State Disability Insurance:	$22.16

3 In which equation is n the total amount of Medicare tax that will be deducted from Barbara's paycheck this year?

A $\dfrac{n}{12} = \$27.44$ 　　　 C $(n)(\$27.44) = 12$

B $(12)(\$27.44) = n$ 　　　 D $\dfrac{\$27.44}{12} = n$

4 A basketball team is averaging 8,184 fans per game for an 82-game season. Thirty percent of the fans at each game buy a hot dog. Which equation could you use to estimate how many hot dogs will be sold this season?

F $B = $ (number of fans per game) $\div$ 82×0.30

G $B = $ (number of fans per game) $+$ 0.30×82

H $B = $ (number of fans per game) $\times$ 82×0.30

J $B = $ (number of fans per game) $\times$ 82×30

5 Renee can run 3 miles in 12 minutes. She went running for an hour and used the equation $3 \times 5 = x$ to calculate how far she ran. What does the x represent?

A the number of miles Renee can run in an hour

B the number of miles Renee runs in 12 minutes

C the number of miles Renee can run in 24 minutes

D the number of miles Renee ran this week

6 In Hawaii, the Kilauea Lighthouse is a wonderful spot to watch dolphins, sea turtles, and whales. The $3 admission price is a real bargain! If $4,011 was paid for admission last week, which expression can be used to find the average number of visitors to the lighthouse each day?

F (total paid) $\times 3 \times 7$

G (total paid) $\div 3 \div 7$

H (total paid) $\div 3 + 7$

J (total paid) $\times 3 \div 7$

7 In the equation $n - 6 = 32$, $n =$

A 26 　　　 C 32

B 38 　　　 D 40

Check your answers on page 125.

An inequality shows when one expression is greater than another. The inequality $9 > 3$ means that 9 is greater than 3. The inequality $4y < 8$ means that four y's are less than 8. Inequalities can usually be solved like equations.

Example Roger is taking Angelica on a date. He wants to spend less than $20. Roger and Angelica spend $11 on dinner. Then Roger decides to buy 2 movie tickets. How much can he pay per movie ticket?

Step 1. Write an inequality that describes the word problem.

$$\$11 + 2t < \$20$$

Step 2. Subtract $11 from both sides of the inequality.

$$\$11 - \$11 + 2t < \$20 - \$11$$

Step 3. Divide both sides of the inequality by 2.

$$\frac{2t}{2} < \frac{\$9}{2}$$

Step 4. Interpret the solution.

$t < \$4.50$ means that Roger can spend up to $4.50 for each movie ticket.

Test Example

Read the question. Circle the answer.

1 The hours that Chin works after school are shown by the expression $5h > 20$. Which describes how many hours Chin works each day?

    A Chin works fewer than 4 hours.

    B Chin works only 4 hours.

    C Chin works more than 4 hours.

    D Chin works fewer than 5 hours.

Hint
The larger part of the inequality sign points to the larger number.

1 C $\frac{5h}{5} > \frac{20}{5}$, so $h > 4$.

Read the questions. Circle the answer.

1 Pat earns less than $800 per week. Which inequality shows Pat's weekly earnings?

A (Pat's earnings) > $800

B (Pat's earnings) > $\frac{$800}{7}$

C (Pat's earnings) < $800

D (Pat's earnings) < $\frac{$800}{7}$

2 Which inequality shows t is greater than 15?

F $t > 15$ H $15\,t > 0$

G $15 > t$ J $t < 15$

3 If $x - 4 < 10$, then

A $x > 6$

B $x < 14$

C $x > 14$

D $x < 6$

4 Eileen can take two suitcases on her trip as long as the weight of the two suitcases is less than 30 kilograms. If w stands for the average weight of her suitcases, which inequality describes Eileen's problem?

F $w > \frac{30}{2}$ H $w < 2 \times 30$

G $2w < 30$ J $2w > 30$

5 It takes Andre more than 15 minutes to run 3 miles. He wrote the inequality $3s > 15$ to calculate how fast he can run. What does the s represent?

A the number of miles Andre runs in an hour

B the number of minutes it takes Andre to run one mile

C the number of minutes it takes Andre to run 3 miles

D the number of miles Andre runs each day

6 The drama club earned more than $1,250 at its last performance. If each ticket cost $3, then which inequality shows t, the number of tickets the drama club sold?

F $$1,250 < t$

G $$1,250 < 3t$

H $$1,250 > t$

J $$1,250 > 3t$

Some of the nutrition information for a new health bar is shown on this table. Study the table and then complete questions 7 and 8.

Nutrient	Percent of Average Daily Requirement
Protein	45%
Vitamin D	> 200%
Starch	25%
Sodium	< 1%

7 Which best describes the amount of vitamin D in the health bar?

A less than twice the average daily requirement

B more than 1% of the average daily requirement

C less than 1% of the average daily requirement

D more than twice the average daily requirement

8 Which best describes the amount of sodium in the health bar?

F less than twice the average daily requirement

G more than 1% of the average daily requirement

H less than 1% of the average daily requirement

J more than twice the average daily requirement

Check your answers on page 125.

Solve. Circle the answer.

1 Sasha can buy 3 cookies for $1.00. She has $5.00 to spend. To find how many cookies she can buy, Sasha uses the equation $3 \times 5 = y$. What does the y in the equation represent?

A the number of cookies she can buy with $3.00

B the greatest number of cookies she can buy

C the amount of money she has

D the amount of money she can spend

2 Which number is a possible solution to the inequality $15 + n < 25$?

F 30 **H** 5

G 40 **J** 12

3 Vivian used $\frac{1}{4}$ cup of milk on her cereal, $\frac{1}{2}$ cup of milk with her cookies, and $\frac{3}{4}$ cup of milk for her sister. How many cups of milk did Vivian use in all?

A $1\frac{1}{2}$ cups

B 1 cup

C $1\frac{1}{4}$ cups

D 2 cups

4 Donuts were on sale at 3 for $2.00. Billy had $8.00 to spend. To find how many donuts he bought, the equation $3 \times 4 = n$ can be used. What does the n in the equation represent?

F the number of donuts Billy bought

G the amount of money Billy had

H the number of donuts Billy bought with $2.00

J the amount of money Billy spent

5 Donna plays tennis for 2 hours on Monday. She plays tennis for the same amount of time 2 other days each week. Which equation can be used to show the amount of time Donna plays tennis each week?

A $2 \times 3 = n$

B $2 + n = 3$

C $3 - 2 = n$

D $n \times 2 = 3$

6 In which equation is n equal to 15?

F $n - 20 = 35$

G $n + 35 = 15$

H $n + 10 = 15$

J $n + 20 = 35$

7 Nina can buy 4 grapefruits for $1.00. She has $3.00 to spend. Nina uses the equation $4 \times 3 = n$. What does n represent?

A the number of grapefruits Nina can buy with $4.00

B the greatest number of grapefruits Nina can buy

C the amount of money Nina has altogether

D the amount of money Nina can spend on grapefruits

8 A recipe that serves 6 people requires 10 ounces of chicken. In which equation is n the total amount of chicken needed to serve 12 people?

F $n = \frac{10}{6} \times 12$

G $\frac{(n)}{12} = 10$

H $(12)(6)(10) = n$

J $\frac{(10)(6)}{6} = n$

9 What number goes in the box to make the number sentence true?

$4 \times 2 \times \square = 40$

A 10

B 6

C 5

D 8

10 Vick starts with 7 and multiplies by 2. Then he keeps multiplying the number he gets each time by 2. What number will he <u>never</u> get?

F 28

G 56

H 112

J 49

11 The table shows "Input" numbers that have been changed by a certain rule to get "Output" numbers. What number is missing from the table?

Input	Output
10	5
24	12
44	22
50	

A 10

B 39

C 25

D 2

12 Tony bought 5 blue pens and 3 black pens. He also bought some red pens. If he bought a total of 10 pens, how many red pens did Tony buy?

F 3

G 2

H 5

J 4

13 The first airplane to fly across the Pacific Ocean averaged more than 85 miles per hour. Which of these inequalities shows how far the airplane likely flew in 6 hours?

A $85 + 6 > \square$

B $85 - 6 > \square$

C $85 \div 6 < \square$

D $85 \times 6 > \square$

14 Nick is planting 5 packets of seeds that contain 20 seeds each. He expects 70% of the seeds to grow into plants. Which equation would you use to find the number of plants Nick can expect to grow?

F $(70 \times 20) \times 0.5 = n$

G $(n \times 20) \times 0.70 = 5$

H $(5 \times 20) \times 0.70 = n$

J $(5 \times 27) \times 0.20 = n$

Check your answers on page 125.

Lesson 19 Appropriate Units

When measuring, choose the most appropriate unit for describing a measurement. Larger measurements can be described in terms such as miles or kilometers. Smaller measurements can be described in terms such as inches or millimeters. For example, it is better to describe the distance between two cities as 560 kilometers instead of 560,000,000 millimeters. The measurement 560,000,000 millimeters also implies that the number of millimeters in the distance is important. In this situation, knowing the distance in kilometers is more useful.

Example An artist has made a giant metal sculpture that is 3 stories tall. Which unit is most appropriate to describe the weight of the unit?

Step 1. Think of units of weight.
Units of weight include (from least to greatest) ounces, pounds, and tons.

Step 2. Think about the size of the object being measured.
A 3-story tall metal sculpture will be very heavy.

Step 3. Choose the appropriate unit.
The most appropriate unit for measuring the weight of the sculpture is tons.

Test Example

Read the question. Circle the answer.

1 Which unit is most appropriate for describing the total land area of your state?

A square inches

B square miles

C square yards

D square feet

1 **B** Because states are large, the best unit to describe their land area is square miles.

Hint

Remember that metric units can be made larger or smaller using multiples of 10.

Read the questions. Circle the answer.

1 Which unit is most appropriate for describing the length of a bumblebee?

A kilometers

B meters

C miles

D millimeters

2 Which measurement is a more convenient way of saying 10,000,000 millimeters?

F 10 kilometers

G 100 kilograms

H 100,000,000 meters

J 20,000,000 inches

3 Which unit is best for describing the capacity of a bathtub?

A gallons

B quarts

C pints

D cups

4 Which unit is best for describing the mass of a paper clip?

F grams

G liters

H kilograms

J tons

5 Which measurement is a more convenient way of saying 63,360 inches?

A 100 feet

B 1 mile

C 5 yards

D 285,120 centimeters

6 Which unit is most appropriate for describing the volume of a house?

F cubic millimeters

G cubic centimeters

H cubic meters

J cubic kilometers

7 Which measurement is most appropriate for describing the distances between baseball bases?

A inches

B feet

C miles

D millimeters

8 Which measurement is a more convenient way of saying 100,000,000 milligrams?

F 10 kilometers

G 1,000,000,000 grams

H 100 kilograms

J 1 ton

Check your answers on pages 125–126.

How much time do you have to eat breakfast before you need to leave for work? Do you have time to buy popcorn before the movie starts? Understanding how to add and subtract time will help you answer daily questions and on the TABE.

Example Diana searched the Internet for $1\frac{1}{2}$ hours to find information about housing prices in her area. If she finished her search at 4:05 p.m., at what time did Diana start searching the Internet?

Step 1. Subtract the time spent searching the Internet (1:30) from the time finished (4:05).

$$\begin{array}{r} 4{:}05 \\ -\ 1{:}30 \\ \hline \end{array}$$

Step 2. Because you can't subtract a larger digit from a smaller, change 4:05 by regrouping. Take 60 minutes (1 hour) from 4 hours to make 3 hours. Then add those 60 minutes to the minutes place. Now subtract.

$$\begin{array}{r} 3{:}65 \\ -\ 1{:}30 \\ \hline 2{:}35 \end{array}$$

Diana started searching the Internet at 2:35 p.m.

Test Example

Read the question. Circle the answer.

1 The digital clock displays below shows when Ben started studying and when he finished. How long did Ben study?

started

finished

Hint

There are 60 minutes in an hour.

A 2 hours and 38 minutes

B 3 hours and 48 minutes

C 3 hours and 38 minutes

D 2 hours and 48 minutes

---

1 **D** Change 7:25 by regrouping. Add 60 minutes to 00:25 and subtract 1 hour from 7:00.

$$\begin{array}{r} {\scriptstyle 6\ \ 7\ 15} \\ 7{:}\cancel{8}\cancel{5} \\ -\ 4{:}37 \\ \hline 2{:}48 \end{array}$$

Applied Math

Read the question. Circle the answer.

The Blakey family is driving from Columbus, Ohio, to Des Moines, Iowa, by way of Chicago, Illinois. The map shows miles and driving times between cities. The time-zone map shows two time zones for the continental United States. Study the map. Then do numbers 1 and 2.

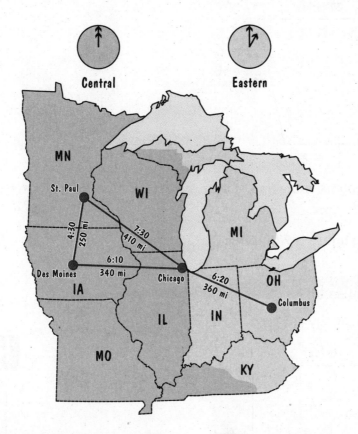

1 According to the map, which of these times is closest to the driving time from Columbus to Des Moines if you travel through Chicago?

A $12\frac{1}{2}$ hours

B $6\frac{1}{2}$ hours

C 17 hours

D 16 hours

2 Mr. Blakey plans to call some friends in Des Moines before the family leaves Columbus. If he calls at 8:30 a.m., what time will it be in Des Moines?

F 6:30 a.m.

G 7:30 a.m.

H 10:30 a.m.

J 9:30 a.m.

Check your answers on page 126.

Lesson 21 Perimeter

Perimeter is the distance around a figure. The length of all the sides are added together to find the perimeter. Some problems on the TABE will involve perimeter.

Example **Pete wanted to find the perimeter of the figure shown below.**

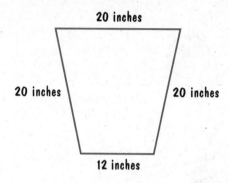

Step 1. Look at the lengths of the four sides.

Step 2. Add to find the perimeter:
20 + 20 + 20 + 12 = 72

The perimeter of the figure is 72 inches.

Test Example

Read the question. Circle the answer.

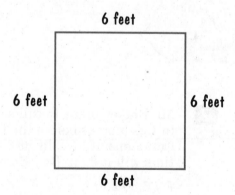

> **Hint**
>
> If all the sides are equal, as in this figure, the perimeter may also be found by multiplying the length of one side by the number of sides.

1 What is the perimeter of this figure?

   A 15 feet

   B 18 feet

   C 24 feet

   D 12 feet

1 **C** The perimeter can be found by adding 6 + 6 + 6 + 6 = 24 feet. You could also multiply 4 sides times the length of each side: 4 × 6 feet = 24 feet.

This diagram shows the dimensions of the Greenes' property. Study the diagram. Then do number 1.

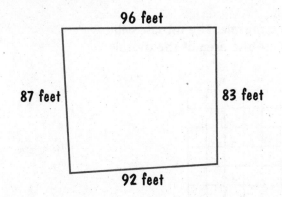

96 feet

87 feet   83 feet

92 feet

1 What is the perimeter of the Greenes' property?

A 397 feet

B 346 feet

C 375 feet

D 358 feet

Read the question. Circle the answer.

2 The borders of Colorado form a rectangle. From north to south, it measures about 280 miles. From east to west it measures 360 miles What is the perimeter of Colorado?

F 1,280 miles

G 1,120 miles

H 720 miles

J 1,140 miles

3 A local soccer field measures about 361 feet by about 246 feet. If you ran around the outside of the soccer field, about how far would you run altogether?

A 607 feet

B 1,214 feet

C 968 feet

D 853 feet

4 A pie was delivered in a square box that has 6-inch sides. What was the perimeter of the box?

F 12 inches

G 18 inches

H 24 inches

J 16 inches

5 The sides of a triangle are 12 inches, 13 inches, and 20 inches. What is the perimeter of the triangle?

A 57 inches

B 33 inches

C 25 inches

D 45 inches

6 What is the perimeter of this figure?

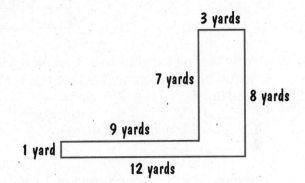

3 yards

7 yards

8 yards

9 yards

1 yard

12 yards

F 40 yards

G 31 yards

H 39 yards

J 50 yards

Check your answers on page 126.

Understanding how to find area is a useful skill. It will help you buy the right number of cans of paint if you are painting a room. You might also need to find the area of a floor to know how much carpeting to buy.

Example Aleta made the grid shown below to plan a mosaic. The mosaic will measure 12 inches by 12 inches. What will be the area of the mosaic in square feet?

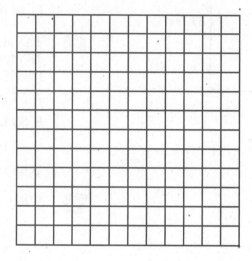

Step 1. Use the formula *Area = length × width* to set up an equation. Express the answer in square units.

$$A = 12 \text{ inches} \times 12 \text{ inches}$$

Step 2. 12 inches = 1 foot. Convert inches to feet.

$$A = 12 \text{ inches} \times 12 \text{ inches}$$
$$= 1 \text{ foot} \times 1 \text{ foot}$$
$$= 1 \text{ square foot}$$

The mosaic will have an area of 1 square foot.

Test Example

Read the question. Circle the answer.

1 The sides of a square are each 24 inches long. What is its area?

    A   24 square feet

    B   4 square feet

    C   24 square inches

    D   4 square inches

Hint

The area of a rectangle is found by using the formula *Area = length × width*. A square is a special type of rectangle.

1 **B** 24 inches = 2 feet. 2 feet × 2 feet = 4 square feet. A square that has sides each measuring 24 inches has an area of 4 square feet.

Read the question. Circle the answer.

1 A carpet measures 8 feet by 10 feet. What is the area of the carpet?

A 18 square feet

B 80 square feet

C 8 square feet

D 60 square feet

2 For the last census, a town was divided into 2-square-mile sections. The town measures 8 miles by 4 miles. If each person covered one section, how many people were needed?

F 16

G 14

H 18

J 32

3 A carpet has an area of 32 square feet. If the length of the carpet is 96 inches, what is its width?

A 4 feet

B 6 feet

C 2 feet

D 8 feet

4 A board measures 24 inches long and 36 inches wide. What is the area of the board?

F 12 square feet

G 60 square inches

H 84 square inches

J 6 square feet

5 Which of these rectangles has the smallest area?

A 6 ft × 10 ft

B 48 in. × 60 in.

C 9 ft × 7 ft

D 120 in. × 84 in.

6 A bag of grass seed will cover an area of 30 square feet. If Sandra's lawn measures 48 inches by 120 inches, how many bags of seed will she need to buy?

F 1

G 2

H 10

J 13

7 A potholder measures 9 centimeters by 8 centimeters. What is the area?

A 9 sq. cm

B 8 sq. cm

C 17 sq. cm

D 72 sq. cm

TABE Strategy

Analyze your mistakes. This will help you avoid repeating them on the TABE.

Check your answers on page 126.

Lesson 23 Rate

Actions are measured in *rates*. For example, a car could be moving at a speed or *rate* of 35 miles per hour. The slope of a mountain could rise at a rate of 100 yards per mile. The interest on a savings account could be 3% per year. The "per" in each of these rates means that one unit is measured in relationship to the other.

Example **A bird flies for 3 hours and travels 36 miles. What is the bird's rate in miles per hour?**

Step 1. Identify the measurements given in the problem: 3 hours and 36 miles

Step 2. Arrange the measurements in the order of the rate. Since the rate is miles per hour, 36 miles belongs before 3 hours.

Step 3. Divide the measurements to get the rate. 36 miles divided by 3 hours gives 12 miles per hour. The bird's rate of flight is 12 miles per hour.

Test Example

Read the question. Circle the answer.

1 A car travels 10 miles in $\frac{1}{4}$ hour. What is the car's rate in miles per hour?

    A   2.5 miles per hour

    B   6 miles per hour

    C   14 miles per hour

    D   40 miles per hour

Hint

The units in the rate must always match the units that are being divided in the problem.

1 **D** 10 miles divided by $\frac{1}{4}$ hour equals $10 \times 4 = 40$ miles per hour.

Read the questions. Circle the answers.

1 Sheila does 30 science problems in 2 hours. What is her rate in problems per hour?

A 60 problems per hour

B 10 problems per hour

C 15 problems per hour

D 28 problems per hour

2 A rocket travels 2,000 miles in 5 minutes. What is its speed in miles per minute?

F 10,000 miles per minute

G 40,000 miles per minute

H   400 miles per minute

J   100 miles per minute

3 A plant grows 3 centimeters every week. What is its rate of growth in centimeters per day?

A $\frac{3}{7}$ centimeters per day

B 21 centimeters per day

C $\frac{7}{3}$ centimeters per day

D $\frac{1}{21}$ centimeters per day

4 The temperature in Whiteville drops 5° Celsius over 10 hours. What is the rate of change in degrees per hour?

F $\frac{2}{5}$ degree per hour

G 5 degrees per hour

H 2 degrees per hour

J $\frac{1}{2}$ degree per hour

5 A bakery produces 25 loaves of bread in $2\frac{1}{2}$ hours. What is its rate in loaves per hour?

A 5 loaves per hour

B 10 loaves per hour

C $\frac{1}{10}$ loaf per hour

D $2\frac{1}{10}$ loaves per hour

6 An airplane flies 500 miles in 2 hours. What is the plane's rate in miles per hour?

F   250 miles per hour

G   300 miles per hour

H 1,000 miles per hour

J   520 miles per hour

7 Water passes over Niagara Falls at a rate of 70,000,000 gallons every 2 minutes. What is the rate of water passing over the falls in gallons per minute?

A   50,000,000 gallons per minute

B   72,000,000 gallons per minute

C   35,000,000 gallons per minute

D 2,100,000,000 gallons per minute

8 On a field trip, Doug sees 10 birds in 5 minutes. At what rate is he seeing birds in birds per hour?

F   60 birds per hour

G 120 birds per hour

H   15 birds per hour

J   50 birds per hour

Check your answers on page 126.

Angles are formed by two lines meeting at an endpoint. Angles are written using the symbol ° or the word "degrees." There are several types of angles. The sum of angles in a triangle is 180°, also written as 180 degrees.

Right angles measure exactly 90°.

Acute angles measure less than 90°.

Obtuse angles measure greater than 90°.

Straight angles measure exactly 180°.

Example   This triangle contains a right angle. If the other two angles are congruent, how many degrees do each of those angles measure?

Step 1. What is the measure of a right angle? A right angle measures 90°.

Step 2. What is the sum of the angles in a triangle? Their sum is 180°.

Step 3. To find the measure of the other 2 angles, subtract the measure of the right angle from the total sum in the triangle: 180° − 90° = 90°.

Step 4. Then divide the remaining sum by 2 since the remaining angles are equal: 90° ÷ 2 = 45°.

Each of the other angles measures 45°.

Test Example

Read the question. Circle the answer.

· **1**   This diagram shows the measure of two angles in a triangle. What is the measure of the third angle?

A   125 degrees

B   86 degrees

C   68 degrees

D   98 degrees

1   B   180 − (69 + 25) = 180 − 94 = 86 degrees.

Applied Math

Read the question. Circle the answer.

1 The diagram shows the measure of two of the angles in the triangle. What is the measure of the third angle?

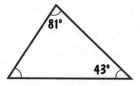

A 56 degrees

B 75 degrees

C 45 degrees

D 47 degrees

2 Jodie's coffee table is triangular in shape. If two of the table's angles measure 36° and 70°, what is the measure of the other angle?

F 94 degrees

G 520 degrees

H 74 degrees

J 254 degrees

3 The diagram shows the measure of two of the angles in the triangle. What is the measure of the third angle?

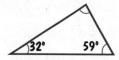

A 91 degrees

B 89 degrees

C 98 degrees

D 88 degrees

4 The triangular stones in a walkway each have two angles that measure 21° and 76°. What is the measure of the third angle?

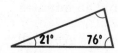

F 97 degrees

G 83 degrees

H 96 degrees

J 180 degrees

Hint

Some people remember the order of angles from least to greatest with this silly sentence:

Always repair older ships.

<90°	Acute
=90°	Right
>90° and <180°	Obtuse
=180°	Straight

Check your answers on page 126.

Solve. Circle the answer.

1 During the first 3 hours of a snowstorm, 6 centimeters of snow fell. At what rate did the snow fall during this period?

A 2 centimeters per hour

B 3 centimeters per hour

C 6 centimeters per hour

D 9 centimeters per hour

2 Ben started jogging at 7:15 a.m. He finished his run at 9:05 a.m. How long did Ben jog?

F 1 hour and 50 minutes

G 1 hour and 40 minutes

H 1 hour and 55 minutes

J 1 hour and 45 minutes

3 Some sunflowers grow taller than people. Which unit would be best to describe the height of these sunflowers?

A centimeters

B meters

C kilometers

D miles

4 A rectangle has a width of 5 centimeters and a length of 10 centimeters. What is the rectangle's perimeter?

F 5 centimeters

G 15 centimeters

H 20 centimeters

J 30 centimeters

5 A room has an area of 132 square feet. Which of these can be the dimensions of the room?

A 12 feet × 11 feet

B 13 feet × 12 feet

C 11 feet × 11 feet

D 14 feet × 12 feet

Maria bought some wooden blocks for her children to play with. This diagram shows the dimensions of one of the blocks. Study the diagram. Then do number 6.

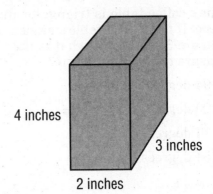

4 inches

3 inches

2 inches

6 What is the area of the front side of this block?

F 6 square inches

G 8 square inches

H 9 square inches

J 14 square inches

7 Jennifer drew a triangle. If two of the triangle's angles measure 30° and 60°, what is the measure of the third angle?

A 45°

B 90°

C 135°

D 180°

8 Birgitta began baking cakes for a bake sale at 6:55 a.m. She finished baking at 11:07 a.m. How long did it take to bake all the cakes?

F 4 hours and 21 minutes

G 4 hours and 12 minutes

H 5 hours and 12 minutes

J 5 hours and 21 minutes

Yolanda wants to travel from Philadelphia to Baltimore by bus. Study the bus schedule. Then answer numbers 9 and 10.

BUS SCHEDULE		
Bus Number	Departure Time	Arrival Time
719	7:20 a.m.	10:35 a.m.
823	9:15 a.m.	11:55 a.m.
611	10:40 a.m.	2:00 p.m.
519	1:05 p.m.	3:45 p.m.

9 Which bus is the slowest?

A 611   C 823

B 719   D 519

10 It takes Yolanda $\frac{1}{2}$ hour to get to the bus station and $\frac{1}{4}$ hour to buy her ticket and get to the departure gate. If she wants to take bus 823, what time should Yolanda leave her house?

F 8:15 a.m.

G 8:45 a.m.

H 8:30 a.m.

J 8:00 a.m.

11 A turtle crawls 100 yards in 4 hours. Which expression shows the rate at which the turtle was crawling?

A 4 yards per hour

B 25 yards per hour

C 104 hours per yard

D 20 hours per year

12 Which unit would be most appropriate for measuring the length of a butterfly?

F inches

G feet

H yards

J miles

13 The students at a read-a-thon read 1,200 pages in 3 hours. Which expression shows the rate at which they read?

A 900 pages per hour

B 4 hours per page

C 90 hours per page

D 400 pages per hour

Check your answers on page 126.

Lesson 25 ▸ Symmetry

When the two halves of a shape look the same, the shape is *symmetrical*. The triangle shown here is symmetrical. If this triangle is folded down the middle on the dotted line, the sides of the triangle will match. This type of symmetry is called *reflection symmetry*.

The octagon shown here has both *reflection symmetry* and *rotation symmetry*. The octagon can be folded on a number of imaginary lines that allow its sides to match. This means it has reflection symmetry. In addition, the shape looks exactly the same when it is given a half turn. When a shape looks the same after a turn, it has *rotation symmetry*.

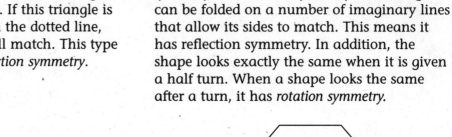

Example What types of symmetry does the circle shown here have?

Step 1. Look for reflection symmetry. The circle can be folded along a vertical line and its sides will match.

Step 2. Look for rotation symmetry. The circle will not look the same when it is turned less than a full turn.

This circle has reflection symmetry, but not rotation symmetry.

Test Example

Read the question. Circle the answer.

1 Which types of symmetry does a square have?

    A only reflection symmetry

    B only rotation symmetry

    C both reflection and rotation symmetry

    D no symmetry

Hint

If a shape shows reflection symmetry in more than one way, it will usually have rotation symmetry also.

1 **C** A square has reflection symmetry across both horizontal and vertical lines. It also looks the same when given a quarter turn.

Read the questions. Circle the answers.

1 Which types of symmetry does the rectangle show?

A only reflection symmetry

B only rotation symmetry

C both reflection and rotation symmetry

D no symmetry

2 Which types of symmetry does this square show?

F only reflection symmetry

G only rotation symmetry

H both reflection and rotation symmetry

J no symmetry

3 Which types of symmetry does this triangle show?

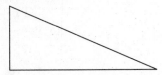

A only reflection symmetry

B only rotation symmetry

C both reflection and rotation symmetry

D no symmetry

4 Which types of symmetry does a circle have?

F only reflection symmetry

G only rotation symmetry

H both reflection and rotation symmetry

J no symmetry

5 Which types of symmetry does this arrow have?

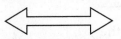

A only reflection symmetry

B only rotation symmetry

C both reflection and rotation symmetry

D no symmetry

6 Which types of symmetry does this pentagon show?

F only reflection symmetry

G only rotation symmetry

H both reflection and rotation symmetry

J no symmetry

7 Which types of symmetry does this shape have?

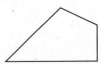

A only reflection symmetry

B only rotation symmetry

C both reflection and rotation symmetry

D no symmetry

8 Which type of symmetry does this shape have?

F only reflection symmetry

G only rotation symmetry

H both reflection and rotation symmetry

J no symmetry

Check your answers on pages 126–127.

You see many shapes each day: a child's blocks, stop signs, yield signs, a baseball diamond, and so on. Knowing the names of these shapes will help you on the TABE.

Any figure with 4 sides is a quadrilateral. A parallelogram is a quadrilateral in which both pairs of opposite sides are parallel. Parallel lines are lines that always stay the same distance apart.

Example **Kendon was asked to name the following shapes.**

A 3-sided figure is a **triangle**.

A **square** has 4 equal sides and is also a parallelogram and a quadrilateral.

A **rectangle** has 4 sides and is also a parallelogram and a quadrilateral.

A 5-sided figure is a **pentagon**.

A 6-sided figure is a **hexagon**.

An 8-sided figure is an **octagon**.

Test Example

Read the question. Circle the answer.

1 What shape is shown below?

A hexagon

B octagon

C quadrilateral

D pentagon

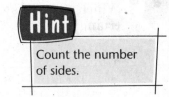

Hint

Count the number of sides.

1 **D** A 5-sided figure is a pentagon.

Read the question. Circle the answer.

1 What kind of a shape is shown below?

A hexagon

B pentagon

C quadrilateral

D octagon

2 Which of these figures is a parallelogram?

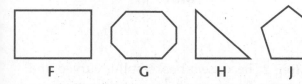

F   G   H   J

3 This famous building is in Washington, D.C. What shape is this building?

A octagon

B pentagon

C rhombus

D hexagon

4 Which of the following is a parallelogram?

F triangle

G octagon

H pentagon

J rectangle

5 Which sign has exactly 2 pairs of parallel lines?

A   B   C   D

6 Loretta drew a figure that was a quadrilateral. Which figure did she draw?

F triangle

G pentagon

H square

J octagon

TABE Strategy

If you finish the test early, use the remaining time to check your answers.

Check your answers on page 127.

Lesson 27 — Solid Figures

There are many types of solid figures you will need to identify on the TABE. You may use some of them every day: ice cubes, cereal boxes, basketballs, and so on.

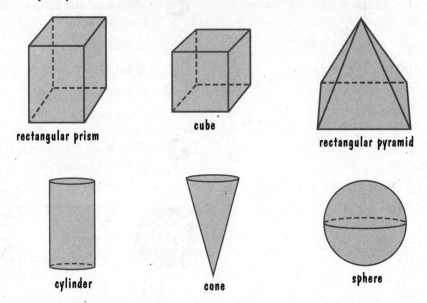

rectangular prism   cube   rectangular pyramid

cylinder   cone   sphere

Example **What shape is a basketball?**

Step 1. Look at the solid figures above.

Step 2. Because a basketball is curved and has no flat surfaces, it must be a sphere.

A basketball is a sphere.

Test Example

Read the question. Circle the answer.

1   What shape is this skyscraper?

A   rectangular prism

B   rectangular pyramid

C   sphere

D   cube

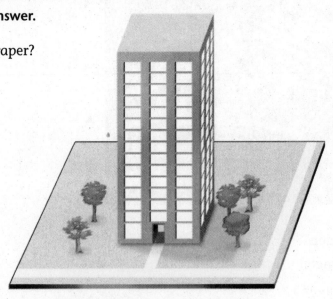

1   **A** Compare the art of this skyscraper to the figures above. This skyscraper is a rectangular prism.

Read the question. Circle the answer.

1 What two solid figures will be formed if the figure is cut along the dotted line?

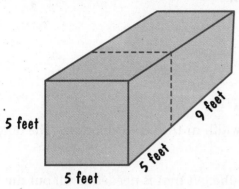

5 feet
9 feet
5 feet
5 feet

A a cube and a rectangular pyramid

B two cubes

C a cube and a rectangular prism

D two rectangular pyramids

2 What shape is Earth?

F a sphere

G a cone

H a triangular pyramid

J a rectangular prism

3 What is the name of this solid figure?

A triangular prism

B cylinder

C rectangular pyramid

D sphere

4 What two solid figures will be formed if the cube is cut along the dotted line?

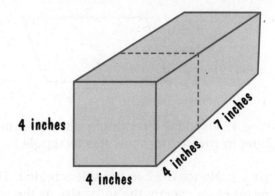

4 inches
7 inches
4 inches
4 inches

F a cube and a rectangular prism

G two rectangular pyramids

H two rectangular prisms

J two square prisms

5 What is a name for the figure?

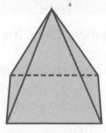

A square prism

B rectangular prism

C rectangular pyramid

D triangular prism

6 What is the difference between a sphere and a cylinder?

F A sphere has two flat surfaces, and a cylinder has none.

G A cylinder is always larger than a sphere.

H A cylinder has two flat surfaces, and a sphere has none.

J The face of a sphere is round, and the face of a cylinder is flat.

Check your answers on page 127.

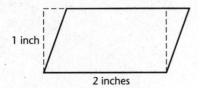 **Lesson 28** **Visualization and Spatial Reasoning**

Visualization is an important tool for solving some mathematics problems. Visualizing a problem can make it easier to estimate or find a solution.

Example **You want to find the area of this parallelogram.**

1 inch
2 inches

Step 1. Visualize a rectangle with the same height and width as the parallelogram. (The dotted lines in the picture show this rectangle.)

Step 2. Notice the two triangles created. The triangle on the left that is needed to fill out the rectangle is exactly the same size as the triangle on the right side of the rectangle.

Step 3. Imagine cutting the triangle on the right side of the rectangle and moving it to make the parallelogram into a rectangle. The area of the figure will not change.

Step 4. Multiply the width of the rectangle by its height to find the area. Its area is 2 square inches. Therefore, the area of the parallelogram is also 2 square inches.

Test Example

Read the question. Circle the answer.

1   Which figure has the greatest area: a circle with a diameter of 2 inches, a square with a width of 2 inches, or a triangle whose longest side is 2 inches?

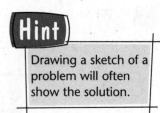

Hint

Drawing a sketch of a problem will often show the solution.

A   the circle

B   the square

C   the triangle

D   not enough information to decide

1   B Drawing a sketch will show that either the circle or the triangle will fit inside the square.

Read the questions. Circle the answers.

1 Sam drew diagonal lines between both sets of opposite corners of a square. What new shapes did his diagonal lines make?

A two rectangles

B three triangles

C four squares

D four triangles

2 Amy has some square tiles. The side of each tile is 1 inch long. How many tiles will she need to make a square with sides 3 inches long?

F 3

G 6

H 9

J 12

3 Carlos is estimating the area of a circle using the following diagram. What would be a good estimate of the area of the circle based on the diagram?

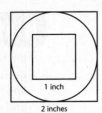

1 inch

2 inches

A between 1 and 2 square inches

B between 2 and 4 square inches

C between 4 and 6 square inches

D between 6 and 10 square inches

4 Rajah cuts up a cube-shaped box along each of its edges. Which shapes does he make?

F 4 rectangles

G 4 squares

H 6 circles

J 6 squares

5 Emilio drew the following triangle. What is a reasonable estimate of the length of the longest side of his triangle?

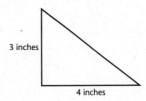

3 inches

4 inches

A 3 inches

B 5 inches

C 8 inches

D 15 inches

6 Louis rolled up a rectanglular piece of paper and stuck circles on the top and bottom of the roll of paper. Which solid shape did Louis make?

F sphere

G pyramid

H cylinder

J cube

7 Peter wants to find the shortest distance from point O to point P. Which of the paths will be shortest?

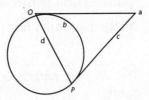

A path a C path c

B path b D path d

8 Jorge is cutting a 3 feet by 1 foot rectangle into 1 foot by 1 foot squares. How many squares will he make?

F 3   H 9

G 6   J none of the above

Check your answers on page 127.

Parallel and Perpendicular

Two lines that make a square corner where they cross are *perpendicular*. Two lines that always stay the same distance apart are *parallel*. *Parallel* lines never cross.

Example Which sides of the square are parallel, and which sides are perpendicular?

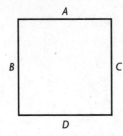

Step 1. Look for lines that stay the same distance apart. Line *A* and Line *D* stay the same distance apart. Line *B* and line *C* also stay the same distance apart.

Step 2. Look for square corners where two lines meet. Line *A* and line *B* make a square corner. Line *A* and line *C*, line *B* and line *D*, and line *C* and line *D* also make square corners.

Lines *A* and *D* and lines *B* and *C* are parallel. Lines *A* and *B*, lines *A* and *C*, lines *B* and *D*, and lines *C* and *D* are perpendicular.

Test Example

Read the question. Circle the answer.

1   The opposite sides of a rectangle do not meet at any corner. These two sides are _____

   A   parallel

   B   perpendicular

   C   parallel and perpendicular

   D   neither parallel nor perpendicular

Hint

If lines *A* and *B* are both perpendicular to line *C*, then lines *A* and *B* are parallel.

1   A The sides are parallel because they stay the same distance apart.

Read the questions. Circle the answers.

**Study the diagram. Then complete
questions 1 through 3.**

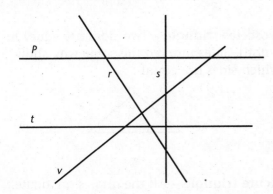

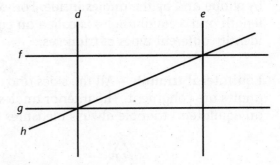

1 Which description fits lines *p* and *r* in
the diagram?

A parallel

B perpendicular

C parallel and perpendicular

D neither parallel nor perpendicular

2 Which description fits lines *s* and *t* in
the diagram?

F parallel

G perpendicular

H parallel and perpendicular

J neither parallel nor perpendicular

3 Which pair of lines is parallel?

A lines *r* and *s*

B lines *p* and *t*

C lines *p* and *s*

D lines *r* and *v*

4 Which description best fits lines *f* and *g*
in the diagram?

F parallel

G perpendicular

H parallel and perpendicular

J neither parallel nor perpendicular

5 Which description best fits lines *f* and *e*
in the diagram?

A parallel

B perpendicular

C parallel and perpendicular

D neither parallel nor perpendicular

6 Which pair of lines is perpendicular?

F lines *f* and *g*

G lines *d* and *e*

H lines *h* and *g*

J lines *e* and *g*

Check your answers on page 127.

Lesson 30 Triangles

Triangles are shapes that have 3 straight lines that are connected. Triangles are classified by shape and by the angles inside. For example, a triangle that has 3 sides that are all the same length and 3 equal angles is called an equilateral triangle. On the TABE you will have to identify different types of triangles.

Equilateral triangle – All the sides and angles are congruent. The interior angles of an equilateral triangle always measures 60°.

Scalene triangle – No sides are equal.

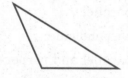

Obtuse triangle – One angle is obtuse.

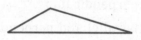

Isosceles triangle – Two sides are equal in length. Sides marked the same way show which sides are equal.

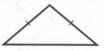

Acute triangle – All the angles are acute.

Right triangle – One angle is a right angle.

No matter what type of triangle, the sum of the angles of a triangle is always 180°.

Example **What kind of triangle is formed by the shape of the vegetable beds shown below?**

No two sides in these triangles are the same length. They each have a right angle.

They can be described as scalene triangles. They can also be called right triangles.

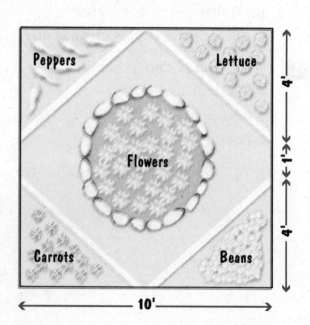

Read the question. Circle the answer.

1 What kind of triangle is formed by the shape of the cabinet in the southwest corner of the room?

　A　right triangle

　B　obtuse triangle

　C　acute triangle

　D　equilateral triangle

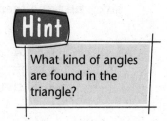

Hint

What kind of angles are found in the triangle?

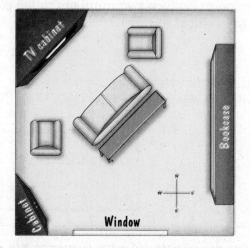

1 **A** This triangle includes a right angle and no two sides are equal. It is a right triangle.

Practice

Read the question. Circle the answer.

1 What is the measure of angle BCA in the triangle?

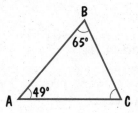

A 60°　　　　　C 66°

B 90°　　　　　D 56°

2 What kind of triangle is shown below?

F obtuse　　　　H right

G scalene　　　　J equilateral

The rectangle below has been divided into triangles. Study the diagram. Then do numbers 3 and 4.

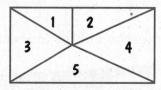

3 How many obtuse triangles are in this figure?

　A 2　　　　　　C 1

　B 0　　　　　　D 3

4 Triangle 3 is an equilateral triangle. What is the measure of each of the angles?

　F 90°　　　　　H 60°

　G 30°　　　　　J 180°

Check your answers on page 127.

Coordinate Geometry

Placing a shape on a measured grid makes it possible to assign numbers to the corners of the shape. Each corner or point is given two numbers called *coordinates*. The horizontal number is given first and then the vertical number.

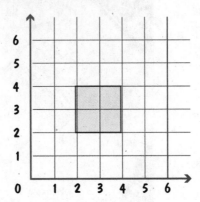

Example **What are the coordinates of each corner of the square shown?**

Step 1. Look at the vertical line passing through the lower-left corner of the square and find its number label. The first number in the coordinate for this corner is 2.

Step 2. Find the number label on the horizontal line passing through the lower-left corner of the square. The second number in the coordinate for this corner is 2. So the lower-left corner of the square has the coordinates (2, 2).

Step 3. Repeat the process to find the coordinates of the upper-left corner, which is (2, 4).

Step 4. Repeat the process to find the coordinates of the lower-right and upper-right corners. The coordinates for the lower-right corner are (4, 2) and the coordinates of the upper-right corner are (4, 4).

The coordinates of the four corners are (2, 2), (2, 4), (4, 2), and (4, 4).

Test Example

Read the question. Circle the answer.

1 What are the coordinates for the point in the center of the square above?

A (3, 3)

B (5, 3)

C (5, 5)

D (3, 5)

Hint

Moving toward the right on the grid, each vertical line adds 1 to the first number in the coordinate pair. Moving upwards the grid, each horizontal line adds 1 to the second number in the coordinate pair.

1 A The center of the square is above the 3 at the bottom of the grid and to the right of the 3 on the left side of the grid.

Read the questions. Circle the answers.

**Study the coordinate grid. Then complete
questions 1 to 3.**

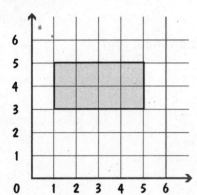

1 What are the coordinates for the upper-
left corner of the rectangle?

A (5, 1)

B (1, 1)

C (1, 5)

D (5, 5)

2 Which are the coordinates for the lower-
right corner of the rectangle?

F (5, 3)

G (5, 5)

H (3, 5)

J (1, 3)

3 How many squares on the coordinate
grid are covered by the rectangle?

A 4

B 6

C 8

D 10

**Study the coordinate grid. Then complete
questions 4 to 6.**

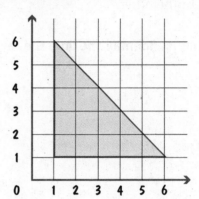

4 Which are the coordinates for the lower-
right corner of the triangle?

F (1, 6)

G (6, 1)

H (1, 1)

J (6, 6)

5 Which are the coordinates for the
upper-left corner of the triangle?

A (6, 1)

B (6, 6)

C (1, 1)

D (1, 6)

6 How many units long is the bottom side
of the triangle?

F 1

G 4

H 5

J 6

Check your answers on page 127.

Lesson 32 Points, Rays, and Lines

In mathematics, a *point* is one location. A *point* is represented by a small circle or dot, but the *point* itself is a location inside the smallest circle. A *line* is a straight path going forever in both directions. A *ray* is a straight path that starts at a point and goes forever in one direction, but not in the other.

Example Identify the line, the ray, and the point on the coordinate grid.

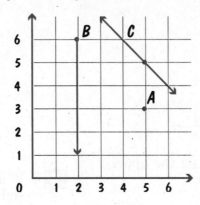

Step 1. Look for the small circle that represents a point. The circle is labeled *A*.

Step 2. Look for a straight path with a circle at one end and an arrow showing it goes forever in one direction. The ray is labeled *B*.

Step 3. Look for the straight path with arrows at both ends showing it goes on forever in both directions. The line is labeled *C*.

Test Example

Read the question. Circle the answer.

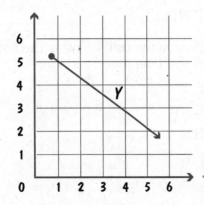

> **Hint**
>
> A ray can be thought of as half a line. Two rays pointing in opposite directions can make a line if they have a common starting point.

1 Which of the following is represented by the path labeled *Y*?

    A   a point   C   a line

    B   a ray   D   none of the above

> **1**   **B**   The straight path with a circle at one end and an arrow at the other represents a ray.

            Applied Math

Read the questions. Circle the answers.

Study the diagram. Then complete questions 1 to 3.

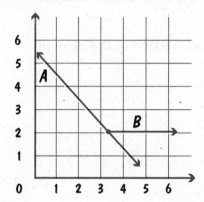

1 Which is represented by the path labeled *A*?

A a point

B a line

C a ray

D none of the above

2 Which is represented by the path labeled *B*?

F a point

G a line

H a ray

J none of the above

3 Which of the following is made where *A* and *B* meet?

A a point

B a line

C a ray

D none of the above

Study the diagram. Then complete questions 4 to 6.

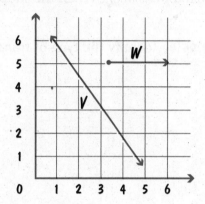

4 Which choice is represented by the path labeled *W*?

F a point

G a line

H a ray

J none of the above

5 Which of the following is represented by the path labeled *V*?

A a point

B a line

C a ray

D none of the above

6 Which best describes the relationship of *V* and *W*?

F *V* and *W* meet at a point on the grid.

G *V* and *W* meet at many points on the grid.

H *V* and *W* meet at a point not on the grid.

J *V* and *W* do not meet.

Check your answers on page 127.

Transformations

A *transformation* is when one shape is changed to make a similar shape. Shapes can go through several different transformations. When the shape is flipped over, it is called a *reflection*. When a shape is turned, it is called a *rotation*. When the shape is moved to a new location, it is called a *translation*. When the shape is made larger or smaller, it is called a *dilation*.

Example Identify the type of transformation shown in each section of the diagram.

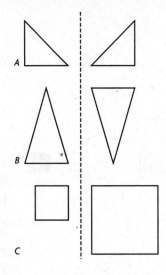

Step 1. Transformation *A* looks like one triangle is reflected in a mirror, so this is a reflection.

Step 2. Transformation *B* shows one triangle has been turned halfway around, so this is a rotation.

Step 3. Transformation *C* shows one square twice as large as the other, so this is a dilation.

Test Example

Read the question. Circle the answer.

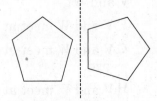

> **Hint**
>
> When a shape is symmetrical, some transformations leave the object unchanged.

1 Which transformation is shown in the diagram?

    A reflection   C translation

    B rotation   D dilation

1 **B** The pentagon has been turned one quarter turn. This is a rotation.

Read the questions. Circle the answers.

Study the diagram. Then complete questions 1 to 3.

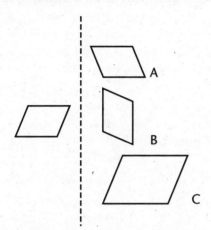

Study the diagram. Then complete questions 4 to 6.

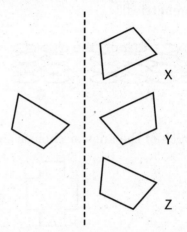

1 Which transformation is shown by shape *A*?

A reflection

B rotation

C translation

D dilation

2 Which transformation is shown by shape *B*?

F reflection

G rotation

H translation

J dilation

3 What transformation is shown by shape *C*?

A reflection

B rotation

C translation

D dilation

4 Which transformation is shown by shape *X*?

F reflection

G rotation

H translation

J dilation

5 What two transformations could be shown by shape *Y*?

A reflection and rotation

B rotation and dilation

C reflection and dilation

D dilation and translation

6 Which transformation is shown by shape *Z*?

F reflection

G rotation

H translation

Check your answers on page 127.

Solve. Circle the answer.

1   Which of the groups of ovals below does <u>not</u> have a horizontal line that will make it symmetrical?

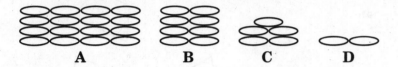

A   B   C   D

2   Which of the answer choices shows a rotation of the figure below?

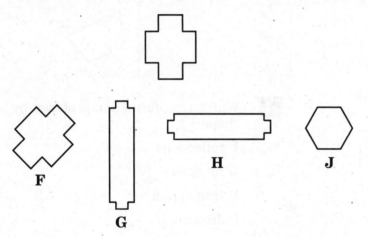

F   G   H   J

3   Each side of a triangle is the same length. What type of triangle is it?

    A right   **B** scalene   **C** obtuse   **D** equilateral

4   Which of these figures is <u>not</u> a parallelogram?

    F   **G**   **H**   **J**

5 What is the measure of the third angle?

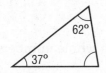

A 118 degrees

B 99 degrees

C 81 degrees

D 261 degrees

6 What kind of triangle is shown in the shape below?

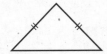

F obtuse

G scalene

H isosceles

J equilateral

7 Which coordinates represent the lower-left corner of the square on the coordinate grid?

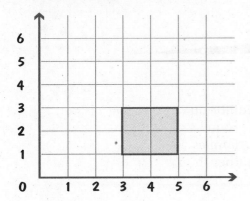

A (1, 3)

B (1, 5)

C (3, 1)

D (3, 3)

8 What kind of triangle is shown in the shape below?

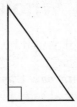

F equilateral   **H** right

G acute   **J** scalene

9 What shape is the figure shown below?

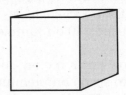

A rectangular pyramid

B cube

C square

D cylinder

10 Which type of transformation is shown in the diagram?

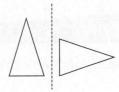

F reflection

G rotation

H translation

J dilation

Check your answers on pages 127–128.

Lesson 34 Whole Numbers in Context

On the TABE you'll be asked to solve many word problems using whole numbers.

Example Jenny saw this advertisement for a special sale. Jenny can spend up to $75. If she buys 8 sample CDs, how many premium CDs can she buy?

CD PRICES

Premium CDs
$15.00 each

Discount CDs
$7.00 each

Sample CDs
$5.00 each

To help solve the problem, Jenny asks herself these questions.

Step 1. How much do sample CDs cost? Sample CDs are $5 each. $8 \times \$5 = \$40$. She will spend $40 on sample CDs.

Step 2. How much money does Jenny have left to spend on premium CDs? $\$75 - \$40 = \$35$. She has $35 left to spend on premium CDs.

Step 3. How much do premium CDs cost? They cost $15 each. How many premium CDs can she buy? $\$35 \div 15 = 2$ with $5 left over.

Jenny can buy 2 premium CDs and have $5 left over.

Test Example

Read the question. Circle the answer.

1 Dan and Angelina want to drive to Monterey, California, from their home in Santa Barbara. The highway route is 216 miles. The scenic route along the ocean is 246 miles. How much farther is it to take the scenic route rather than the highway route?

    A 276 miles   C 30 miles

    B 132 miles   D 45 miles

1 C Subtract 246 (length of the longest route) − 216 (length of the shortest route) = 30 miles more to take the scenic route.

Read the question. Circle the answer.

1 Mark wanted to install a fence around his yard. How many 6-foot sections of fencing will be needed to put a fence on the north side of the yard?

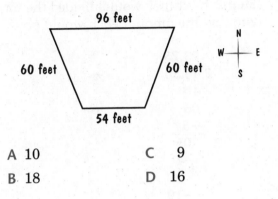

96 feet

60 feet   60 feet

54 feet

N
W ─┼─ E
S

A 10   C 9
B 18   D 16

The Greene family is driving from Miami, Florida, to Atlanta, Georgia. The map below shows the miles they will drive. Study the map. Then do number 2.

Driving Distance Map

2 How many miles will the Greene family drive if they go from Miami to Atlanta through Jacksonville?

F 793 miles   H 820 miles
G 810 miles   J 723 miles

This graph shows the change in temperature in New York City on May 29. Study the graph. Then do numbers 3 and 4.

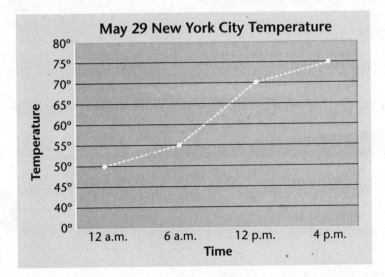

3 What is the difference between the temperature at 12 a.m. and 4 p.m.?

A 15°   C 25°
B 20°   D 10°

4 What is the difference between the temperature at 6 a.m. and 12 p.m.?

F 10°   H 20°
G 25°   J 15°

Check your answers on page 128.

Lesson 35) Decimals in Context

Some problems on the TABE will ask you to add, subtract, multiply, and divide decimals.

Example Dan and Angelina went to dinner. The bill was $40.00, and they decided to leave a $6.50 tip. If they split the bill, how much did each of them pay?

Step 1. First they would add the tip of $6.50 to the bill of $40.00.

$$\begin{array}{r} \$40.00 \\ + \ \$6.50 \\ \hline \$46.50 \end{array}$$

Step 2. Next they would divided the total by 2 to find the amount each would pay.

$$\begin{array}{r} 23.25 \\ 2\overline{)46.50} \\ \underline{-4} \\ 06 \\ \underline{-6} \\ 05 \\ \underline{-4} \\ 10 \\ \underline{-10} \\ 0 \end{array}$$

Each must have paid $23.25.

Example Casper is painting his fence. It stands 10 feet tall and is 50 feet long. A can of exterior paint costs $26.70 per gallon. Each gallon will cover 400 square feet. What would be the total cost of the paint needed to paint the fence?

Step 1. Find the total area that needs to be painted. Remember that you find area by multiplying length × width. The answer will be in square feet. 50 × 10 = 500 square feet. Because 1 can of paint will cover only 400 square feet and Casper needs to cover 500, he will need 1 can for the first 400 square feet of fence and 1 can more to finish.

Step 2. To find the total cost of the paint, multiply the cost of a can times the number of cans needed, which is 2.

$$\begin{array}{r} {\scriptstyle 1\ 1} \\ \$26.70 \\ \times \qquad 2 \\ \hline \$53.40 \end{array}$$

The cost of paint for Casper's fence will be $53.40.

Test Example

Read the question. Circle the answer.

1 Tim rode 15.5 miles on his bicycle to the park yesterday. What is the distance in kilometers that Tim rode to the park?

A 9.61 km

B 25 km

C 16.12 km

D 14.88 km

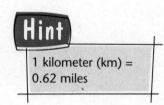

Hint

1 kilometer (km) = 0.62 miles

1 **B** Divide total miles (15.5) by the number of miles in 1 km (0.62). 15.5 ÷ 0.62 = 25

Read the question. Circle the answer.

1 The Brown family is making 10 cakes for a school bake sale. Each cake will contain chocolate chips. One bag of chocolate chips is enough for 2 cakes. If each bag costs $2.99, how much will the chocolate chips cost?

A $11.96

B $17.94

C $8.97

D $14.95

2 Ted ran in a 3.1 mile race. What is the distance in kilometers that Ted ran?

(1 kilometer [km] = 0.62 miles)

F 3.72 km

G 5 km

H 1.922 km

J 2.48 km

Clark kept track of his monthly expenses. The chart shows some of his expenses. Study the chart. Then do number 3.

Monthly Expenses

Rent	$865.75
Electric	$78.16
Entertainment	$49.70
Telephone	$30.95
Apartment Insurance	$61.85

3 Clark earns $1978.64 per month. After deducting all of his expenses listed here, how much does Clark have left to spend?

A $875.90

B $921.56

C $892.23

D $982.32

4 It is 3.7 miles from Keifer's farm into town. How far is the distance in kilometers?

(1 kilometer [km] = 0.62 miles)

F 2.29 km

G 4.32 km

H 5.97 km

J 3.08 km

5 Jack took his wife to a baseball game. Each ticket cost $12.75 and Jack paid with two $20 bills. How much change did Jack receive?

A $27.00

B $14.50

C $25.50

D $12.75

6 Wendy needs 12 windows for her house. Each window will need 10 feet of aluminum to finish it. The aluminum comes in 30-foot rolls. If each roll costs $9.53, how much will the aluminum cost?

F $38.12

G $114.36

H $95.30

J $28.59

Check your answers on page 128.

In each window box Sam planted $\frac{1}{4}$ package of flower seeds. If he has $\frac{3}{4}$ package of flower seeds, he can plant seeds in 3 containers.

Many problems on the TABE involve multiplying and dividing fractions. To multiply fractions, multiply the numerators of each fraction. Then multiply the denominator.

$$\frac{1}{3} \times \frac{2}{5} = \frac{2}{15}$$

To divide fractions, reverse the numerator and denominator of the second fraction and change the operation sign to multiplication. Then multiply the fractions.

$$\frac{3}{4} \div \frac{1}{4} \text{ becomes } \frac{3}{4} \times \frac{4}{1} = \frac{12}{4} = 3$$

To change a whole number to a fraction, put the whole number over a 1.

$$1 = \frac{1}{1}, 4 = \frac{4}{1}, 15 = \frac{15}{1}, \text{ and so on.}$$

Example Ken plans to study for $1\frac{1}{2}$ hours each day for his GED. The test is in 12 days. How many hours will Ken be studying?

Step 1. Change $1\frac{1}{2}$ to a fraction. Multiply the denominator by the whole number. Add the numerator of the fraction to the result: $2 + 1 = 3$. Put this result over the original denominator of the fraction.

Step 2. Multiply by the number of days:

$$\frac{3}{2} \times \frac{12}{1} = \frac{36}{2}$$

Step 3. Simplify the fraction by dividing the numerator by the denominator.

$$36 \div 2 = 18$$

Ken will study for 18 hours.

Test Example

Read the question. Circle the answer.

1 Rosa has 50 pieces of candy. She ate $\frac{1}{10}$ of the candy on the way home from the store. She divides the rest of the candy among 5 people. How many pieces of candy does each person get?

    A 8

    B 9

    C 6

    D 7

1 **B** First multiply 50 by $\frac{1}{10}$ to find how many pieces of candy Rosa ate. $\frac{50}{1} \times \frac{1}{10} = \frac{50}{10}$. Simplify the fraction to $\frac{5}{1}$ or 5. Rosa ate 5 pieces of candy. Then subtract the candy she ate from the total amount of candy: $50 - 5 = 45$. Rosa had 45 pieces left to split among 5 people. Now divide the candy that is left by the number of people: $45 \div 5 = 9$. Each person gets 9 pieces of candy.

Practice

Read the question. Circle the answer.

1 Phil is buying bags of cement to repair his sidewalk. Each bag of cement weighs $23\frac{1}{2}$ pounds. How many pounds of cement will Phil have if he buys 3 bags?

A $69\frac{1}{2}$ pounds   C 68 pounds

B $70\frac{1}{2}$ pounds   D $73\frac{1}{2}$ pounds

Carlos wants to put ceiling tiles in his den. This diagram shows the dimensions of the den. Study the diagram. Then do number 2.

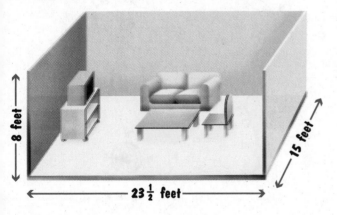

2 Each ceiling tile covers $2\frac{1}{2}$ square feet. What is the minimum number of ceiling tiles Carlos will need to cover the ceiling of his den?

F 200   H 152

G 146   J 141

Cathy is making meatloaf for her family. This list shows the ingredients for a recipe that will serve 4 people. Study the recipe. Then do numbers 3 and 4.

Ingredients
1½ pounds ground beef
¼ cup chopped onion
½ cups breadcrumbs
2 eggs, beaten
1 8-ounce can tomato sauce

3 If Cathy wants to double the recipe, how many pounds of ground beef will be needed?

A 4 pounds   C 3 pounds

B $2\frac{1}{2}$ pounds   D $3\frac{1}{2}$ pounds

4 Cathy wants to make a smaller meatloaf for lunch. If she cuts the recipe in half, how much breadcrumbs will Cathy use?

F $\frac{1}{6}$ cup   H $\frac{1}{4}$ cup

G $\frac{2}{3}$ cup   J $\frac{5}{6}$ cup

Check your answers on page 128.

Tina was ordering plants from a mail-order nursery. The details below explain the shipping charges. Study the explanation. Then do numbers 1 and 2.

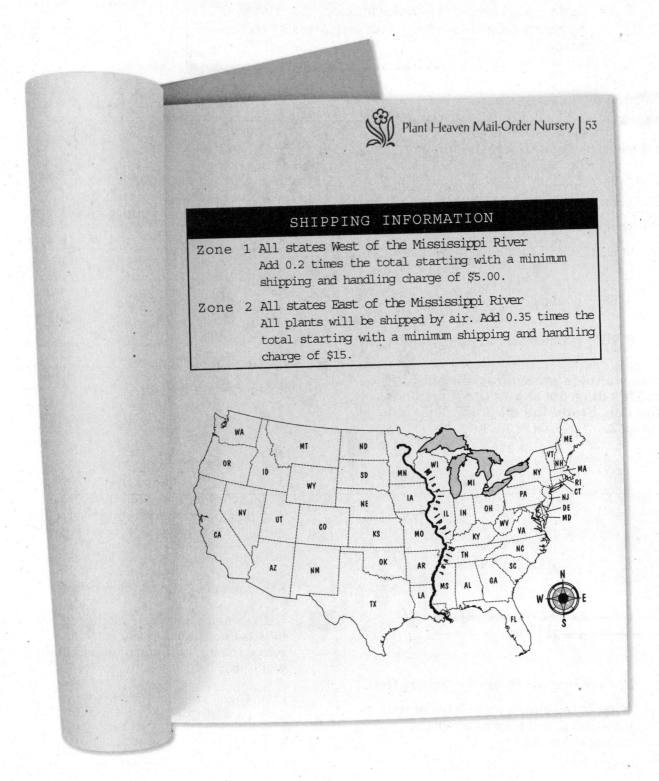

Plant Heaven Mail-Order Nursery | 53

SHIPPING INFORMATION

Zone 1 All states West of the Mississippi River
Add 0.2 times the total starting with a minimum shipping and handling charge of $5.00.

Zone 2 All states East of the Mississippi River
All plants will be shipped by air. Add 0.35 times the total starting with a minimum shipping and handling charge of $15.

1. Tina lives in Pennsylvania (PA). If she ordered $80 worth of plants, what is her total cost?

   A $118

   B $28

   C $102

   D $108

2. The nursery was running a sale and all orders over $100 received a $12 discount. If Joe wanted $120 worth of plants shipped to his home in Arizona (AZ), how much did he pay?

   F $131.80

   G $129.60

   H $127.90

   J $135.00

3. Sheila went for a 9-mile hike. If she wanted to take a break after each $\frac{3}{4}$ of a mile, how many breaks did she take?

   A 9

   B 12

   C 6

   D 14

The intensity, or loudness, of sound is measured in decibels. The chart below shows the decibel levels of certain sounds. Study the chart. Then do numbers 4 and 5.

Loudness

Sound	Decibels
Breathing	10
Street traffic	?
Subway	100
Jet Airplane	140

4. The decibel level of street traffic is $\frac{1}{2}$ of the decibel level of a jet airplane. What is the decibel level of a street traffic?

   F 7

   G 70

   H 0.7

   J 77

5. A sound with a decibel level 1.2 times greater than the decibel level of a subway can cause pain in the ear. What decibel level would cause discomfort?

   A 120 decibels

   B 60 decibels

   C 140 decibels

   D 80 decibels

Check your answers on page 128.

Lesson 37 Reasonableness of an Answer

A reasonable answer is one that makes sense. The numbers fit the situation. If you recognize that an answer isn't reasonable, you know you have to rethink the solution to the problem.

Example Susan works out with weights. She lifts a 10-pound weight 10 times during each of her workouts. She told her friend, Dawn, that if she worked out 10 days in a row, she would lift a total of 100,000 pounds. Is Susan correct?

Step 1. Think about the numbers in the problem. 100,000 pounds is a lot of weight to lift in only 10 days.

Step 2. Plan a solution. Ask yourself: How could I figure out how much Susan would have to lift each day for 10 days to reach 100,000 pounds?

Step 3. Do the math. 100,000 ÷ 10 = 10,000. Susan would have to lift 10,000 pounds each day to reach 100,000 pounds.

Susan is incorrect. Lifting a 10-pound weight 10 times a day will take 1,000 days (about 3 years) to add up to 100,000 pounds.

Example The trunks of most trees increase by about 1 inch in circumference per year. At this rate, Jordan said it would take a tree about 300 years to increase its trunk size by 1 foot. Is Jordan's answer reasonable?

Step 1. Think about the numbers in the problem.
- The growth rate is 1 inch per year.
- Jordan is estimating how long it will take for the tree to increase its trunk 1 foot in circumference. There are 12 inches in a foot.
- 300 years is a long time. Not many trees live to this age.

Step 2. Plan a solution. Ask yourself: How could I figure how long it would take for a tree trunk to increase by 1 foot? Multiply the growth rate times the number of inches in a foot.

Step 3. Multiply. 1 inch per year × 12 inches = 12 years

Jordan's answer is not reasonable. 300 years is much too long.

Read the question. Circle the answer.

1 Mike works 20 days a month at his job. If he earns about $80 per day, what is the best estimate of about how much Mike earns in a month?

A $60,000

B $16,000

C $160

D $1,600

Hint

If you simplify a multiplication problem by removing the 0's, don't forget to rewrite them in your answer.

1 **D** Remove the two 0's to simplify the problem. Multiply $2 \times 8 = 16$. Now rewrite the two 0's to the end of 16, and Mike's monthly earnings are about $1,600.

Practice

Read the question. Circle the answer.

1 About 60 families live in the Bermuda Town development. The area of the development is 10 square miles. About how many families are there per square mile?

A 6,000

B 600

C 6

D 60

2 Alex had 10 pieces of lumber for his project. He measured only 3 pieces of lumber. Which of these is the best estimate of the fraction of lumber Alex measured?

F between $\frac{1}{3}$ and $\frac{1}{2}$

G between $\frac{1}{4}$ and $\frac{1}{3}$

H between $\frac{2}{3}$ and $\frac{3}{4}$

J between $\frac{1}{2}$ and $\frac{2}{3}$

3 Kelli runs about 5 miles round trip to and from the park, 3 days each week. At the end of 20 weeks, what is the best estimate of about how far Kelli had run?

A 3,000 miles

B 30 miles

C 300 miles

D 30,000 miles

4 Jackson needs to place a classified ad in the local newspaper. Each 1-inch space of text costs $4.00 for 14 days. If Jackson has $13.00, about how many inches of text can he buy?

F 3 inches

G $3\frac{1}{2}$ inches

H 56 inches

J $10\frac{1}{4}$ inches

Check your answers on page 128.

Lesson 38 — Whole Rounding

Rounding is an estimation technique. When you round, you replace the numbers in the original problem with compatible numbers to make a simpler problem.

Example Ben plans to refurnish his house. He has $5,000.00 to spend. If his plans call for spending $1,257.00 on his living room, $675.52 on his bathroom, and $2,340.50 on his bedroom, will he have approximately enough money to get what he wants?

Step 1. Round each of the numbers to the nearest hundred. Look for the rounding number—the digit to the right of the place to which you are rounding. If this digit is less than 5, the digit to its left does not change. If this digit is 5 or greater, add 1 to the hundreds place. Change all digits to the right into 0s.

The digit to the right of the hundreds place is in the tens place.

1,257.00 rounds to 1,300.00. The rounding number is 5 or greater, so the 2 rounds to 3.
675.52 rounds to 700.00. The rounding number is 5 or greater, so the 6 rounds to 7.
2,340.50 rounds to 2,300.00. The rounding number is less than 5, so the 3 does not change.

Step 2. Add the rounded numbers. 1,300 + 700 + 2,300 = 4,300.

Ben will spend about $4,300.00. He will have enough money.

Example Which of these numbers when rounded to the nearest tenth is the same number when rounded to the nearest whole number?

   3.865   3.813   4.469   4.023

Step 1. Round each of the numbers to the nearest tenth. The rounding number is in the hundredths place.

number	nearest tenth
3.865	3.9
3.813	3.8
4.469	4.5
4.023	4.0

Step 2. Round each of the numbers to the nearest whole number. The rounding number is in the tenths place.

number	nearest whole number
3.865	4
3.813	4
4.469	4
4.023	4

Step 3. Compare. 4.0 = 4

To the nearest tenth, 4.023 rounds to 4.0; to the nearest whole number, 4.023 also rounds to 4.

Read the question. Circle the answer.

1 How many numbers in the box will be 220,000 when
rounded to the nearest ten thousand?

| 228,421 | 218,100 | 225,001 | 215,013 |

A 1   C 3

B 2   D 4

---

1 **B** The 4 numbers, rounded to the nearest ten thousand, are
230,000; 220,000; 230,000; and 220,000. The second and
fourth numbers round to 220,000.

Practice

Read the question. Circle the answer.

Isaac earns $1,654.90 per month. The table
shows the state and federal deductions
that are subtracted from his monthly
paycheck. Study the table. Then do
number 1.

FEDERAL DEDUCTIONS	
Federal Income Tax:	$198.32
Social Security Tax:	$102.15
Medicare Tax:	$25.04

STATE DEDUCTIONS	
State Income Tax:	$24.89
State Unemployment Insurance and State Disability Insurance:	$23.44

1 After all federal and state deductions
are taken out, Isaac's net monthly
income is about

A $1,230.00

B $1,000.00

C $1,500.00

D $1,330.00

2 Which of these numbers when rounded
to the nearest tenth is the same number
when rounded to the nearest whole
number?

F 5.985

G 5.799

H 6.158

J 5.813

3 Which of these numbers, when rounded
to the nearest tenth, is the same
number as when rounded to the nearest
whole number?

A 1.973

B 1.789

C 1.652

D 2.079

Check your answers on page 128.

Lesson 39 Estimation

There are many ways you use estimation every day. You use estimation when thinking about how much you can spend at the grocery store, how much gas you can buy, how long it will take you to finish a project, and so on. When you are asked to estimate an answer, you will find an approximate answer rather than an exact answer.

Example Marcia works as a landscape designer. The diagram shows her plan for a new client's backyard. If a 1-pound bag of fertilizer covers an area of 225 square feet, about how many pounds of fertilizer will be used to cover the back lawn?

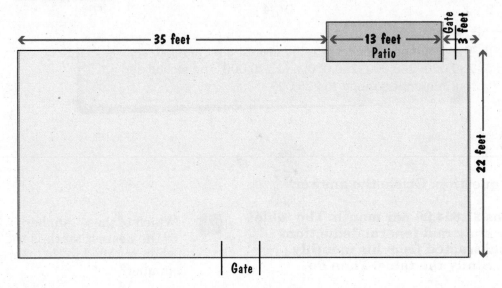

Step 1. Figure the approximate length and width of the backyard.
Length = 35 + 13 + 3 = 51 feet, which rounds to 50.
Width = 22 feet, which rounds to 20.

Step 2. Figure the approximate area. $A = l \times w$.
$50 \times 20 = 1,000$ square feet.

Step 3. Figure the number of fertilizer bags needed.
Round 225 square feet to 200 square feet and divide.
$1,000 \div 200 = 5$

Marcia will need about 5 pounds of fertilizer.

Test Example

Read the question. Circle the answer.

1   Marcia's design includes 20 shrubs. The price of each shrub is $46.92. Which of these is the best estimate of the total cost of the shrubs?

A $3,000

B $2,000

C $1,000

D $4,000

1 **C** You can round $46.92 to $50.00. Then multiply by 20, the number of shrubs. $50.00 × 20 = $1,000.00.

Practice

Read the question. Circle the answer.

Study this advertisement for a custom-built bookcase. Then do number 1.

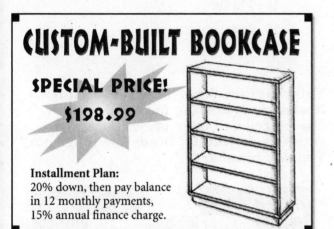

CUSTOM-BUILT BOOKCASE

SPECIAL PRICE!

$198.99

Installment Plan:
20% down, then pay balance
in 12 monthly payments,
15% annual finance charge.

1 The regular price is 20% more than this special price. Which of these is the best estimate of the regular price of the bookcase?

A $220

B $270

C $240

D $230

2 If there are 19 dozen people in a movie theatre, about how many people are in the movie theatre?

F 150

G 100

H 250

J 300

3 The regular price for sapling maple trees at Barnes Nursery is $62.80. The trees are 25% off the regular price this week. Which of these is the best estimate of the sale price of the trees?

A $25

B $55

C $45

D $35

4 This chart shows the number of new voters who registered over the last seven weeks. Which of these is the best estimate of the average number of new voters that registered?

New Voters

Week	How Many
1	209
2	95
3	163
4	164
5	84
6	135
7	132

F 150

G 160

H 170

J 140

TABE Strategy

The word *about* signals that the answer should be an estimate.

Check your answers on pages 128–129.

1 There is an average of 20 students per class in the Smith Middle School. There are 30 classes in the school. How many students attend Smith Middle School?

A 60

B 600

C 6,000

D 6,060

2 How many numbers in the box will be rounded to 160,000 when rounded to the nearest ten thousand?

| 154,523 158,047 153,979 154,608 |

F 1

G 2

H 3

J 4

3 Shares of stock in a company were selling for $41.25 per share. The price of a share dropped 10% last week. Which of these is the best estimate of the new price for a share of stock?

A $36

B $38

C $32

D $34

4 Vic went grocery shopping with his 20%-off-everything-in-the-store coupons. He bought orange juice for $1.69, breadcrumbs for $2.29, and eggs for $1.29. Which of these is the best estimate of how much money Vic saved by using his coupons?

F $1.00

G $3.00

H $4.00

J $2.00

This diagram shows plans for a quilt Roshanda is making for her daughter. The pieces will have grey, black, and white backgrounds. Study the diagram. Then do number 5.

5 Which of these is the best estimate of the fraction of the quilt that is covered by black pieces?

A between $\frac{1}{4}$ and $\frac{1}{3}$

B between $\frac{1}{3}$ and $\frac{1}{2}$

C between $\frac{1}{2}$ and $\frac{2}{3}$

D between $\frac{2}{3}$ and $\frac{3}{4}$

Applied Math

6 Helen can run a half-mile in 4 minutes. She can run 2 miles in about how many minutes?

F   5 minutes

G   16 minutes

H   8 minutes

J   10 minutes

7 Steve reads that a local TV shop is marking down all DVD players by 18% from the regular price. If a DVD player usually sells for $89.95, about how much can Steve save by buying the DVD player on sale?

A $10.00

B $30.00

C $18.00

D $25.00

8 Which of these numbers, when rounded to the nearest tenth, is the same number when rounded to the nearest whole number?

F   4.767

G   4.902

H   4.951

J   3.069

9 Gretchen earns $1,858.46 per month. After deductions of $201.36, $109.32, $27.54, $22.11, and $34.17, her monthly income is about

A $1,000

B $1,400

C $1,600

D $1,500

10 A 60-pound bag of concrete mix will cover 10 square feet. About how many bags will be needed to cover an area of 147 square feet?

F   14

G   15

H   16

J   17

11 The regular price of bicycles at Main Street Bike Shop is $159.95. This week, the bicycles are on sale for 25% off the regular price. Which of these is the best estimate of the sale price of the bicycles?

A $135

B $130

C $120

D $125

Check your answers on page 129.

Lesson 40 ▸ Solve Problems

Before solving any problem, it is important to know what steps will lead to a solution. Determine what information is needed and decide how to get that information. Some problems require several steps before a solution is reached.

Example **Aaron has half as many marbles as Brigitte. Caleb has five times as many marbles as Aaron. If Caleb and Aaron put all their marbles together, they would have 120 marbles. How many marbles does Brigitte have?**

Step 1. Decide what steps will lead to a solution. To find the amount of marbles Brigitte has, we need to know how many marbles Aaron has. To find how many marbles Aaron has, we need to use the information that is given. We know that the number of Aaron's marbles plus 5 times that number equal 120.

Step 2. Since the number of Aaron's marbles plus 5 times that number equals 120, they can be combined. Therefore, six times Aaron's marbles equals 120. Aaron has $\frac{120}{6}$ marbles.

Step 3. Dividing 120 by 6 shows that Aaron has 20 marbles. Brigitte has twice that many marbles or 2×20.

Brigitte has 40 marbles.

Test Example

Read the question. Circle the answer.

1   The size of the math club doubles every year. Three years ago the math club had 21 members. Which steps will lead to finding the size of the math club this year?

A   dividing 21 by 3 to find the number of members per year

B   finding the number of members two years ago and last year

C   finding the number of members the club will have next year

D   multiplying 21 by 3 to find how many members the club has for three years

Hint

Write down everything that you know or find out about a difficult problem. Check your notes to see what information is helpful.

1   **B** Multiply 21 by 2 to find the number of members 2 years ago. Then multiply by 2 again to find the number of members last year. Finally, multiply by 2 to find the number of members in this year's club.

Read the questions. Circle the answers.

1 The Aqua Blue Music Store sold 300 CDs this week. Half of the CDs were sold on Friday and Saturday. The number of CDs sold on Saturday was twice as much as the number sold on Friday. Which step will lead to finding how many CDs were sold on Friday?

A calculating how many CDs were sold on Thursday

B calculating how many CDs were sold on Friday and Saturday

C calculating the profit the store made over the week

D dividing 300 by 7 to find the average number of CDs sold each day

2 Maria and her two friends spent $48 at the movies. They paid $8 each for tickets. They also shared $6 worth of popcorn and two ice cream bars costing $3 each. They spent the rest of their money on 3 drinks. Which step will lead to finding how much one drink costs?

F dividing $48 by 3 to find out how much each friend paid

G adding $8, $6, and $3 to find the cost of a ticket, popcorn, and ice cream

H subtracting the known costs from $48 to find how much 3 drinks cost

J adding $48 plus the amount the friends paid for tickets to get the total expenses

3 The mean of Kim's grades in History is 83. Kim had 8 different grades, and the total of 7 of his grades is 575. Which step will lead to finding Kim's other grade?

A multiplying 83 by 8 to find the total of all Kim's grades

B subtracting 83 from 575 to find the total of six of Kim's grades

C dividing 575 by 83 to find the number of tests Kim has taken

D adding 8 and 7 to find how many more tests Kim will take

4 The sum of the degree measures in three angles is 180°. Two of the angles have the same degree measure. The third angle measures half of 180° degrees. Which step will lead to finding the degree measure of the two identical angles?

F dividing 180° by 3 to find the average of the angle degree measures

G dividing 180° by 2 to find the measure of the third angle

H multiplying 180° by 1.5 to find the total of four angles

J multiplying the degree measure of the identical angles by 3 to get the total degree measure of the triangle

5 Mr. Jackson took a survey to determine the number of pets owned by all the students in his class. He found that there were $3\frac{1}{2}$ pets per student. If there are 12 boys and 10 girls in the class, which steps will lead to finding how many total pets the students own?

A adding the number of boys and girls and multiplying by $3\frac{1}{2}$

B subtracting the number of girls from the number of boys and adding 3

C multiplying $3\frac{1}{2}$ by 12 and adding 10

D dividing $3\frac{1}{2}$ by 10 and multiplying by 12

6 It took 8 hours for Inez to travel from Miami to Chicago. She spent 1.5 hours getting to the airport, 2 hours waiting for her plane, and the rest of the time in the air. If it is 1,187 miles from Miami to Chicago, which steps will lead to finding her plane's average speed?

F subtracting 2 and 1.5 from 8 and dividing 1,187 by the result

G dividing 1,187 by 8 and subtracting 2 plus 1.5

H multiplying 2 times 1.5 times 8, then dividing by 1,187

J none of the above

Check your answers on page 129.

Missing, Extra Information

Chuck is in charge of setting up the tables for his club's dinner. Each table can seat 12 people. He wants to set up the tables the night before the dinner. How many tables will he need? Before Chuck can set up the correct number of tables, he needs to know how many people will be attending the dinner. Before you can solve problems, you may need to find missing information. Once you have all your information, you can make a plan to find a solution.

Example **Read the word problem. What information do you need to answer the question? Flights leave New York every 45 minutes to fly to Boston. If the first flight is at 6:00 a.m., when will the fifth flight of the day arrive in Boston?**

Step 1. What is being asked? *When will the fifth flight of the day arrive in Boston?*

Step 2. What information do you have? *Flights leave every 45 minutes. The first flight is at 6:00 a.m.*

Step 3. Is that enough information to answer the question? *No.*

Is there is any information missing? **Yes, you need to know how long the flight from New York to Boston lasts in order to answer the question.**

Test Example

1 **A new apartment complex has 10 buildings. What information is needed to find the maximum number of apartments that can be rented?**

   A the number of empty apartments

   B the number of people who want to rent

   C the number of apartments in each building

   D the number of floors in each building

Hint

What is the question? Which facts are needed to solve the problem?

---

1 **C** You know there are 10 buildings. You need to know how many apartments are in each building before you can find the maximum number of apartments that are available to rent.

TABE Strategy

Sometimes word problems have extra information that you don't need to solve the problem. Read word problems carefully to decide what information is necessary to solve the problem.

Read the question. Circle the answer.

1 A basketball arena has 65 rows of seats. What information is needed to find the number of people the arena can seat?

A number of people at each game

B number of empty seats per game

C number of seats in each row

D number of rows in each section

2 There are 5 performances of a play at the Civic Center. An equal number of tickets were sold to each performance. What information is needed to find out how many tickets were sold for each?

F the total number sold

G the time of the performance

H the number of performances a day

J the location of the Civic Center

3 This chart shows two of the tallest buildings in the world. If you added the Sears Tower, which information would you need to find the average height of the 3 buildings?

Building	Height
Petronas Tower I	1,483 feet
CN Tower	1,804 feet

A height of the Sears Tower

B number of stories in CN Tower

C year the Petronas Tower was built

D height of CN Tower

4 Tony wanted to buy hamburger buns and 3 pounds of hamburger meat. The meat cost $2.69 per pound, and a package of buns cost even more. To find the total Tony spent, which information do you need?

F the cost of the meat

G the amount of meat Tony bought

H the cost of the buns

J the distance to the grocery store

5 The planet Neptune has 8 known moons. Pluto has 1 known moon. Saturn has many more known moons. What information is needed to find out how many moons the 3 planets have in all?

A Saturn's distance from the Sun

B time each moon takes to orbit Saturn

C the number of Saturn's known moons

D the names of the Neptune's moons

6 In 1999, 638,000 refugees entered the United States. Fewer refugees entered Canada the same year. What information is needed to find how many refugees entered both countries?

F the population of Canada

G how many refugees entered Canada

H the year of the statistic

J countries the refugees came from

7 Ted wanted to buy 14-inch pizzas for his friends. Each of his friends will eat 2 slices and there are 10 slices in each pizza. What information is needed to find the number of pizzas Ted will order?

A how many slices each friend will eat

B the number of Ted's friends

C how the pizza is cut

D the size of the pizza

8 Tim made a phone call that cost $2.50 for the first minute and $0.25 for each additional minute. Which information is needed to find the cost of the call?

F the number of phone calls he made

G how long he was on the phone

H how long he has owned the phone

J the time of day the call was made

Check your answers on page 129.

Evaluate Solutions

Sometimes the "solution" to a problem does not make any sense. If a calculator indicates that 6 times 7 equals 3, either the calculator is broken or the problem was entered incorrectly. In the same way, if the "solution" to a problem indicates that 12 inches is equal to 500 miles, something has gone wrong. Inches are a smaller unit than miles. This is why it is important to evaluate each solution to make sure that it makes sense.

Example **Theodore was working on this problem.**
"Divide 20 hot dogs between 5 people."
He got the answer "100 hot dogs per person". How should he evaluate this solution?

Step 1. Think, "Is it reasonable that 20 hot dogs divided between 5 people is 100 hot dogs per person?" Can each person have more hot dogs than the total number of hot dogs there were originally?

Step 2. If the solution is not reasonable, ask what may have gone wrong. In this case, Theodore multiplied by 5 instead of dividing.

Step 3. Try an alternate solution and see if this solution is more reasonable: $20 \div 5 = 4$. Think, "Is it reasonable that 20 hot dogs divided between 5 people is 4 hot dogs each?" In this case, each person gets less than a quarter of the total. This solution is more reasonable.

Test Example

Read the question. Circle the answer.

1 Jeff was doing the problem $4b + 5 = 21$. His solution was $b = \frac{1}{4}$. Evaluate the reasonableness of his solution to the problem.

   A This is a reasonable solution since 4 times $\frac{1}{4}$ equals 1.

   B This is not a reasonable solution because $4b$ should equal 16.

   C This is not a reasonable solution because b must be greater than 26.

   D This is not a reasonable solution because b should equal 0.

Test each solution in the original problem and see if the solution works.

1 **B** Since $4b + 5 - 5 = 21 - 5$, $4b$ should equal 16.

Read the questions. Circle the answer.

1 Delores spent $10 for 5 cartons of milk. She calculated that she spent $5 per carton. Evaluate the reasonableness of her solution to the problem.

A This is a reasonable solution because $5 plus 5 cartons equals $10.

B This is not a reasonable solution because $5 times 5 equals $25.

C This is not a reasonable solution because the price should be $15 per carton.

D This is not a reasonable solution because 5 cartons divided by $10 equals $0.50 per carton.

2 Tom calculated that the probability of flipping two coins and having both land on heads was 150%. Evaluate the reasonableness of his solution.

F This is a reasonable solution because the probability of each coin landing on heads is 50%.

G This is not a reasonable probability because only one coin can land on heads.

H This is not a reasonable solution because the probability should be twice 100%.

J This is not a reasonable solution because there should never be probabilities greater than 100%.

3 Keith calculated that the mean of the numbers 15, 20, 16, and 19 was 8. Evaluate the reasonableness of his solution.

A This is a reasonable solution because 8 is twice 20 minus 16.

B This is not a reasonable solution because the mean should be an odd number.

C This is not a reasonable solution because the mean should be between 15 and 20.

D This is not a reasonable solution because the mean should equal 20 minus 15.

4 Neal solved the inequality $3x > 9$. His solution was that x is less than 3. Is his solution reasonable?

F Yes, because 9 divided by 3 is 3.

G No, because the problem tells what x is greater than, not what x is less than.

H No, because 9 minus 3 equals 6.

J No, because x should be less than 12.

5 Malory calculated how much money she would have if she saved $10 a week for 10 weeks. Her solution was $700. Is this solution reasonable?

A Yes, because Malory saved every day for ten weeks.

B No, because 10 times 10 equals 100.

C No, because $700 is less than the amount Malory wants to save.

D No, because $700 divided by 10 weeks equals $10.

6 Regina drove 200 miles in 8 hours. She calculated that she drove an average of 25 miles per hour. Is her solution reasonable?

F Yes, because 8 times 25 is 200.

G No, because the speed limit is 55 miles per hour.

H No, because 200 divided by 8 equals 50.

J No, because 25 times 8 is 300.

Check your answers on page 129.

1 Kristen solved the problem $2x - 3 = 11$. Her solution was $x = 14$. Evaluate the reasonableness of her solution to the problem.

   A This is a reasonable solution because 11 plus 3 equals 14.

   B This is not a reasonable solution because 2 times 14 minus 3 equals 25.

   C This is not a reasonable solution because x must be greater than 33.

   D This is not a reasonable solution because x should equal 1.

2 Randy solved the problem $4x + 3 > 7$. He came up with the solution $x > 40$. Is his solution reasonable?

   F Yes, because 4 times 40 plus 3 is greater than 7.

   G No, because the number x is greater than should be less than 10.

   H No, because x should be less than a number.

   J No, because x should equal 0.

3 Jose wanted to buy apples for each of the guests at his party. He wanted to have 2 apples for each guest. Which information is needed to find how many apples Jose should buy?

   A how many apples each guest will eat

   B how many guests will come to the party

   C how much the apples cost

   D when the party will take place

4 Dan, Elena, and Keiko all collect postcards. Dan has twice as many postcards as Elena does, and Keiko has twice as many postcards as Dan does. If Elena and Dan combined their postcards, they would have 150 in all. Which steps will lead to finding how many postcards Keiko has?

   F Multiply 150 by 2 to know how many postcards Keiko has.

   G Multiply 150 by $\frac{2}{3}$ to know how many postcards Dan has, then multiply by 2.

   H Divide 150 by 3 to know how many postcards Elena has and then multiply by 2.

   J Multiply 150 by 2 to find how many postcards Dan has, then divide by 3.

5 Brad bought a book that normally sold for $18 at a 20% off sale. The clerk said that the sale price was $20. Evaluate the reasonableness of this price.

   A This is a reasonable price because $18 + 2 = $20.

   B This is not a reasonable price because 20% off of $20 is not $18.

   C This is not a reasonable price because $20 is not 20% of $18.

   D This is not a reasonable price because the sale price should be less than the normal price.

6 The size of the Music Town Chorus increases by $\frac{1}{2}$ every year. Two years ago the chorus had 30 members. Which steps will lead to finding the size of the chorus this year?

F Find the number of chorus members last year and then multiply by 1.5.

G Find the number of chorus members two years from now and then divide by 3.

H Find the number of chorus members there were three years ago and then add 100.

J Find how many more chorus members there are each year and then multiply by the number of years.

7 Emily read 10 books last month. What information is needed to find out how many pages she read?

A how long it took her to read each book

B what type of books she read

C the number of pages in each book

D the price of each book

8 A city theater held 10 performances of a new play. The average price of a ticket to the performances was $25, and all the tickets were sold for each performance. Which information is needed to find the total revenue for the performances?

F the number of tickets to each performance

G the length of each performance

H the population of the city

J the number of empty seats at each performance

9 Alberto calculated that the mean of the numbers 13, 19, 14, and 16 was 52. Evaluate the reasonableness of this solution.

A This is a reasonable solution because 52 is about 4 times 14.

B This is not a reasonable solution because the mean must be an even number.

C This is not a reasonable solution because the mean should be between 13 and 19.

D This is not a reasonable solution because the mean should equal 19 minus 13.

10 Ramona spent $25 for 3 magazines. She calculated that she had spent $22 for each magazine. Evaluate the reasonableness of her solution.

F This is a reasonable solution because $25 minus 3 equals $22.

G This is not a reasonable solution because $25 times 3 equals $75

H This is not a reasonable solution because the price should be $28 for each magazine.

J This is not a reasonable solution because the price per magazine should be $\frac{1}{3}$ of $25.

11 Mr. Hermez drove 400 miles in 10 hours. He calculated that he drove an average of 80 miles per hour. Is his solution reasonable?

A Yes, because the speed limit is 65 miles per hour.

B No, because 80 times 10 is 800.

C No, because 400 times 10 is more than 80.

D No, because 10 divided by 400 is $\frac{1}{40}$

Check your answers on pages 129–130.

The Applied Math Assessment is identical to the real TABE in format and length. It will give you an idea of what the real test is like. Allow yourself 50 minutes to complete this assessment. Check your answers on pages 130–131.

Sample A

What number is missing from this number sequence?
3, ____, 7, 9, 11

A 2

B 4

C 5

D 6

---

1 If you start with 6, then multiply that number by 3, and then keep multiplying the number you get each time by 2, you will <u>never</u> get which number?

A 144

B 72

C 288

D 96

2 Which sampling method would produce a random sample of the students at Renee's school?

F interviewing 10 of Renee's friends

G interviewing the members of the honor society

H interviewing every 5 students outside the school entrance

J interviewing 25 students in the chess club

3 Which of these is another way to show 403?

A $(4 \times 100) + (3 \times 10)$

B four hundred three

C $40 + 3$

D 4 hundreds 3 tens

4 In which inequality below must r be greater than 20?

F $r - 5 < 25$

G $r + 10 > 20$

H $r - 20 < 40$

J $r + 5 > 25$

5 The graph shows the amount of money taken in at two major league baseball games in 1 night. Which of these statements is true?

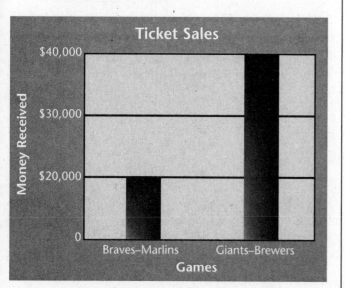

A The Giants–Brewers game took in half as much money as the Braves–Marlins game.

B The Braves–Marlins game took in $15,000 more fans than the Giants–Brewers game.

C The Giants–Brewers game took in twice as much money as the Braves–Marlins game.

D The Braves–Marlins game took in one-third less than the Giants–Brewers game.

6 A school gym has 20 rows of seating. What information is needed to find the maximum number of students who can sit in the gym?

F the number of students attending the school

G the number of students in each grade

H the number of students each row can seat

J the number of windows in the gym

7 The price of a TV is $350. If a 6% sales tax is added to this price, what is the total cost of the TV?

A $21.00

B $371.00

C $329.00

D $325.00

8 Which of the coordinates show the upper-left corner of the square?

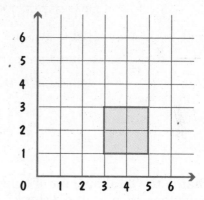

F (3, 3)

G (5, 3)

H (3, 5)

J (5, 5)

Andy earns $1,995.75 per month. This table shows the federal and state deductions that are subtracted from Andy's monthly paycheck. Study the table. Then do numbers 9 through 12.

```
FEDERAL DEDUCTIONS

Federal Income Tax:                              $235.04

Social Security Tax:                             $117.52

Medicare Tax:                                     $29.38


STATE DEDUCTIONS

State Income Tax:                                 $37.29

State Unemployment Insurance
  and State Disability Insurance:   $23.73
```

9 What is the total amount of federal deductions from each paycheck?

  A $381.94

  B $367.76

  C $385.64

  D $377.14

10 Andy pays 1% of his monthly income in extra health coverage. To compute this amount, he must multiply $1,995.75 by

  F 0.01

  G 1.0

  H 0.001

  J 0.1

11 In which equation is n the total amount of state income tax that will be deducted from Andy's paycheck this year?

  A $\dfrac{\$37.29}{12} = n$

  B $\dfrac{\$1,995.75}{n} = 12$

  C $(n)\,(\$37.29) = 12$

  D $(12)\,(\$37.29) = n$

12 After all federal and state deductions are taken out, Andy's net monthly income is about

  F $1,400

  G $1,800

  H $1,600

  J $1,300

Pam ordered a cedar chest for storing her clothes. This diagram shows the dimensions of the chest. Study the diagram. Then do numbers 13 through 16.

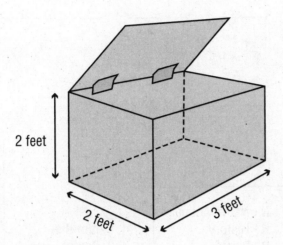

2 feet

2 feet

3 feet

13 A 2-inch line in the diagram represents a 3-foot edge of the chest. What scale was used to draw the diagram?

A 1 inch = 1 foot

B 1 inch = $1\frac{1}{2}$ feet

C 1 inch = 2 feet

D 1 inch = $\frac{1}{2}$ foot

14 Pam decided to order a larger cedar chest with the same proportions as the cedar chest shown in the diagram. The height of the larger cedar chest will be 36 inches. What will be the length and width of the larger cedar chest?

F 54 inches × 36 inches

G 54 inches × 30 inches

H 48 inches × 36 inches

J 48 inches × 30 inches

15 Pam bought 3 sheets of special paneling to protect the inside of the chest. Each sheet costs $12.95. The sales tax is 6%. What is the total cost of the paneling? (Round to the nearest cent.)

A $41.89

B $40.78

C $42.03

D $41.18

16 How many square feet of paneling would it take to cover the bottom of a chest that is 2 feet by 3 feet?

F 4 square feet

G 6 square feet

H 10 square feet

J 15 square feet

This diagram shows the plans for a new visitors center at the wildlife park. Study the diagram. Then do numbers 17 through 21.

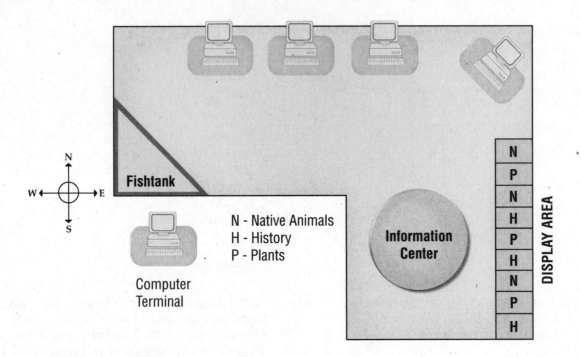

Fishtank

N - Native Animals
H - History
P - Plants

Computer
Terminal

**Information
Center**

DISPLAY AREA

N
P
N
H
P
H
N
P
H

17 Each computer takes an average of 7 minutes to install. About how long did it take to install all the computers?

A $\frac{1}{2}$ hour

B 1 hour

C 1 $\frac{1}{2}$ hours

D 2 hours

18 There will be information windows spread around the Information Center. If the windows are at 3-foot intervals, what measurement would be most convenient to determine the number of information windows needed?

F the radius

G the area

H the circumference

J the diameter

19 The workers spent $\frac{1}{2}$ of their time installing carpeting, $\frac{1}{4}$ of their time painting, $\frac{1}{3}$ of their time finishing the roof, and $\frac{1}{9}$ of their time cleaning up. The workers spent the greatest amount of time

A   cleaning up

B   installing carpeting

C   finishing the roof

D   painting

20 What kind of triangle is formed by the fish tank in the southwest corner?

F   equilateral

G   obtuse

H   scalene

J   right

21 What fractional part of the display area is devoted to native animals?

A $\frac{1}{2}$

B $\frac{1}{3}$

C $\frac{1}{4}$

D $\frac{2}{3}$

22 Which number could replace the variable x to make the equation true?

$1 \times 2 \times x = 10$

F   10

G   5

H   25

J   2

23 Which of these decimals is less than 0.916 and greater than 0.906?

A   0.910

B   0.903

C   0.921

D   0.905

24 The table shows "Input" numbers that have been changed to "Output" numbers by applying a specific rule. What number is missing from the table?

Rule: Multiply by 2, then subtract 5.

Input	Output
6	7
8	11
11	?
15	25

F   19

G   15

H   13

J   17

25 Which of these figures is <u>not</u> a quadrilateral?

A   B   C   D

This map shows the trails for Harriman Park. Study the map. Then do numbers 26 through 29.

Harriman Park

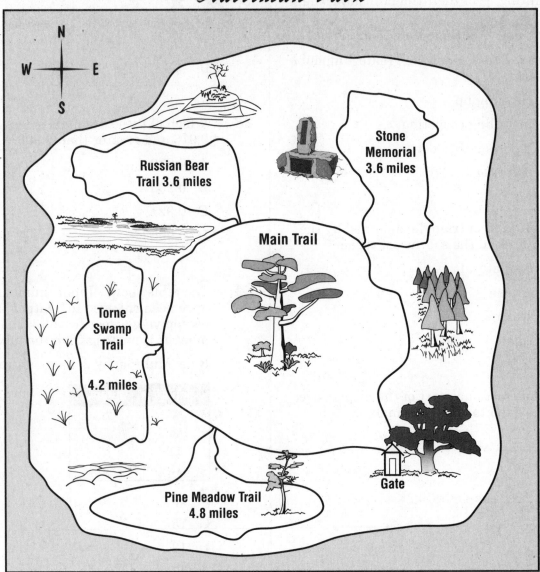

TABE Fundamentals: Applied Math

26 The distance around Stone Memorial is what fraction of the distance around Pine Meadow?

F $\frac{3}{4}$

G $\frac{1}{2}$

H $\frac{2}{3}$

J $\frac{1}{3}$

27 What is the distance in kilometers around Torne Swamp?

(1 kilometer = 0.62 miles)

A 2.49 km

B 6.77 km

C 5.95 km

D 1.53 km

28 Which of these is another way to write the distance around the Pine Meadow Trail?

F $4\frac{1}{2}$ miles

G $4\frac{8}{10}$ miles

H four and eight-hundredths miles

J 4 and two-fifths miles

29 It takes about 10 minutes to hike $\frac{1}{4}$ mile. How long will it take to hike the Russian Bear Trail?

A 2 hours 10 minutes

B 2 hours 40 minutes

C 1 hour 20 minutes

D 2 hours 24 minutes

30 Which of these numbered triangles is similar to triangle ABC?

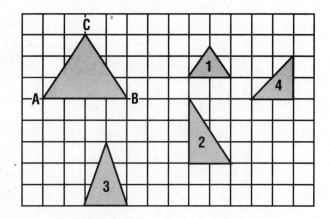

F triangle 1

G triangle 2

H triangle 3

J triangle 4

31 How many numbers in the box will be 130,000 when rounded to the nearest thousand?

| 131,499 | 124,426 | 129,612 | 123,789 |

A 1

B 2

C 3

D 4

32 Which of these numbers when rounded to the nearest tenth is the same number when rounded to the nearest whole number?

F 8.923

G 8.799

H 9.095

J 8.973

Mr. James plans to put a gravel walkway around his property. This diagram shows the dimensions of the James' property. Study the diagram. Then do numbers 33 through 36.

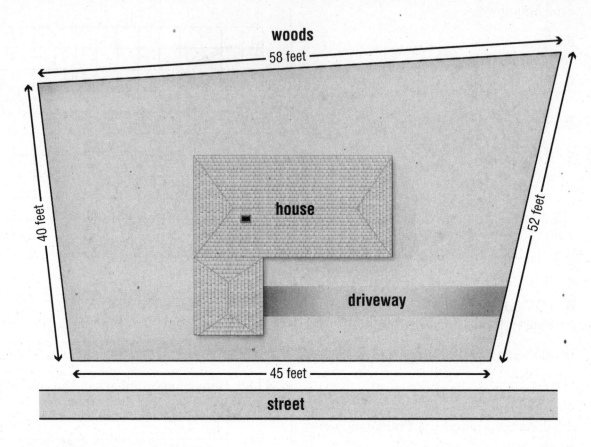

33 The walkways will be 3 feet wide. Which of these is another way to describe the walkway?

   A about 50 inches wide

   B about 1 meter wide

   C about 2 yards wide

   D about 2 meters wide

34 What is the perimeter of the James' property?

   F 195 feet

   G 215 feet

   H 165 feet

   J 235 feet

35 There will be 6 birdfeeders scattered around the backyard. Every 2 birdfeeders will require a 50-pound bag of birdseed. If each bag of birdseed costs $8.75, how much will the birdseed cost?

   A $28.25

   B $35.00

   C $17.50

   D $26.25

36 There will also be a sidewalk placed between the property and the street. If the sidewalk is divided into 5-foot sections, how many sections will there be?

   F 10

   G 7

   H 9

   J 8

Go On ▶

This circle graph shows the expenses of a company. Study the graph. Then do numbers 37 through 40.

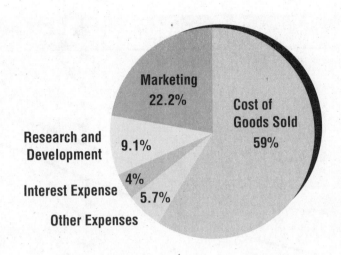

37 According to the graph, for every $100,000 of income, how much is spent on interest expense?

    A $400

    B $40,000

    C $4,000

    D $400,000

38 The company recorded these expenses for one week. Which of these equations shows a way the company can use these expenses and the information in the graph to estimate their interest expense (E) for a year?

    F E = (total expenses for one week) ×
       52 − 0.04

    G E = (total expenses for one week) ×
       52 ÷ 0.04

    H E = (total expenses for one week) ×
       52 × 0.04

    J E = (total expenses for one week) ×
       12 ÷ 0.04

39 According to the graph, if the company totals its marketing, interest expense, and research and development expenses, what percent of the total expenses does this represent?

    A 35.3%

    B 36.3%

    C 34.3%

    D 37.3%

40 Last month, the cost of goods was $70,000. This month the company has reduced expenses in this area by 30%. How much did the company spend this month for the cost of goods sold?

    F $59,000

    G $40,000

    H $49,000

    J $91,000

This graph shows monthly normal temperatures from January through May for selected cities. Study the graph. Then do numbers 41 through 44.

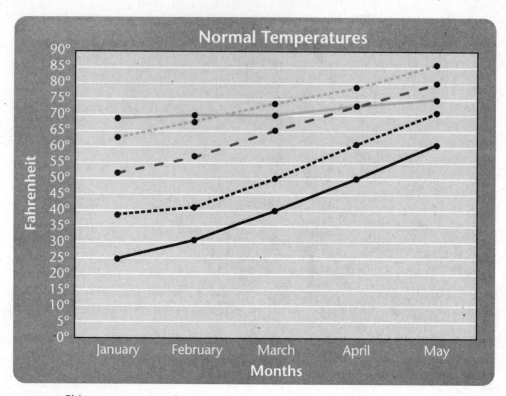

Normal Temperatures

Months

——— Chicago
▪▪▪▪▪▪ New York
——— Los Angeles
▪▪▪▪▪ Houston
— — Atlanta

41 According to the graph, which city had the greatest increase in temperature from April to May?

A Los Angeles

B Chicago

C Atlanta

D Houston

42 Which two cities have average temperatures below 65° in four of the five months?

F New York and Chicago

G Chicago and Los Angeles

H New York and Atlanta

J Houston and Chicago

43 In May, the average temperatures from least to greatest are in

A Chicago, New York, Los Angeles, Houston, Atlanta

B New York, Chicago, Los Angeles, Atlanta, Houston

C Houston, Atlanta, Los Angeles, New York, Chicago

D Chicago, New York, Los Angeles, Atlanta, Houston

44 Which of these is the best estimate of the average temperature for all 5 cities in March?

F 55°   **H** 60°

G 50°   **J** 70°

TABE Fundamentals: Applied Math

The Smith family is going on their family vacation. They are using a road map that uses a scale of 1 inch = 30 miles. Using this information, do numbers 45 through 49.

45 What fraction of an inch equals 15 miles?

A $\frac{1}{8}$

B $\frac{1}{4}$

C $\frac{1}{3}$

D $\frac{1}{2}$

46 If the Smiths drive 120 miles, how many inches will this be on the map?

F 3 inches

G 2 inches

H 4 inches

J 5 inches

47 Gasoline costs $1.89 per gallon. How much will 10 gallons of gasoline cost?

A $189.00

B $18.90

C $1,890.00

D $1.89

48 The Smith family needs to drive 300 miles. They have already driven $\frac{1}{3}$ the distance. If they drive the remaining distance in 4 hours, what is their average speed?

F 50 miles per hour

G 60 miles per hour

H 30 miles per hour

J 40 miles per hour

49 The scale of the map is changed to 1 inch = 40 miles. Using an actual distance of 240 miles, how would the number of inches on the map be changed?

A It would decrease by 2 inches.

B It would increase by 3 inches.

C It would increase by 2 inches.

D It would decrease by 4 inches.

50 Which type of transformation is shown by the triangles?

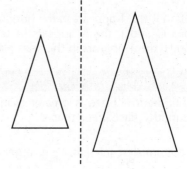

F rotation

G reflection

H translation

J dilation

STOP ✳

Lesson 1 Practice (page 9)

1. C four hundred eight thousand two hundred fifty-six is the same as 408,256.

2. F Three hundred seven is the same as 307.

3. D 2,797 is the same as two thousand seven hundred ninety-seven.

4. G $(8 \times 100) = 800$; $(4 \times 10) = 40$. $800 + 40 = 840$.

5. A Fifty thousand ninety-three is the same as 50,093.

6. F Four hundred seven is the same as 407.

Lesson 2 Practice (page 11)

1. B The 4 appears in the tens place. The 4 stands for $4 \times 10 = 40$.

2. J The 5 appears in the hundredths place. The 5 stands for $5 \times \frac{1}{100} = \frac{5}{100}$.

3. B In option B, the 2 is in the hundreds place. In options A and C, the 2 is in the tens place. In option D, the 2 is in the ones place.

4. G In option G, the 6 is in the tenths place. In options F and J, the 6 is in the hundredths place. In option H, the 6 is in the ones place.

5. C In option C, the 5 is in the hundredths place. In options B and D, the 5 is in the tenths place. In option A, the 5 is in the ones place.

6. G The 4 appears in the hundreds place. The 4 stands for $4 \times 100 = 400$.

7. B The 7 appears in the ones place. The 7 stands for $7 \times 1 = 7$.

8. F In option F, the 1 appears in the hundreds place. In options G and J, the 1 appears in tens place. In option H, the 1 appears in the ones place.

Lesson 3 Practice (page 13)

1. C The hundredths place is greater than 2, and the thousandths place is less than 8.

2. H $\frac{3}{5}$ is the smallest fraction. $\frac{3}{4}$ is larger than $\frac{3}{5}$ and smaller than $\frac{7}{8}$. $\frac{7}{8}$ is a little smaller than 1, and $\frac{7}{6}$ is larger than 1. $\frac{9}{7}$ is the largest fraction.

3. D First, look at the tenths. Then look at hundredths places.

Lesson 4 Practice (page 15)

1. A Find the east section. There are 6 equal sections. Of the 6 sections, 2 are luxury seating. $\frac{2}{6}$ can be rewritten as $\frac{1}{3}$.

2. G Netz Place is 0.8 miles in length and Willets Road has a length of 2.4 miles. The top and bottom numbers of $\frac{0.8}{2.4}$ may be divided by 0.8, which results in the fraction $\frac{1}{3}$.

Lesson 5 Practice (page 17)

1. B Each of the points on the number line is 0.01 apart.

2. J Each of the points on the number line is 0.01 apart.

3. A Each of the points on the number line is 0.02 apart.

4. F Each of the points on the number line is 0.04 apart.

5. A Each of the points on the number line is .02 more than the point to its left. One point to the left of 0.49 is 0.47.

6. J There are two segments on the number line between 0.55 and 0.57. The difference between these numbers is 0.02 This tells you that each segment of the number line represents 0.01 ($0.02 \div 2 = 0.01$). The box is four segments up the number line from 0.57.
$0.57 + 4(0.01) = 0.57 + 0.04 = 0.61$.

7. B Wednesday is the only day in the chart with a snowfall amount of 0.06 inches.

8. J Each point on the number line is .01 apart. The box is at 0.10.

Lesson 6 Practice (page 19)

1. B Setting up the scale as a fraction $\frac{2}{6}$, we see the ratio is 1 inch = 3 feet when we reduce the fraction.

2. J The ratio of the length of Stan's patio to Sarah's is 22:11 or 2. The width of Sarah's patio is 10 feet. If this ratio is applied, the width of Stan's patio will be 20 feet.

Lesson 7 Practice (page 21)

1. A Multiply $\$95.99 \times 0.07 = \$6.72$ sales tax on each CD player. If each CD player will cost $102.71 ($95.99 + $6.72), then 2 CD players will be $205.42 ($102.71 × 2).

2. H 5% is written as 0.05 in decimal form.

3. B 20% of $30 is $6 (30 × 0.20), so the special rate is $24 ($30 − $6). This rate is multiplied by 103 hours to find the cost of $2472 for snow removal.

4. F 6% of $50 is $3 (50 × 0.06 = $3). This is added to $50 for the full cost of $53.

5. D 20% of $53 is $10.60 ($53 × 0.20).

Lesson 8 Practice (page 23)

1. D 7+(8+2)=(7+8)+2 The parentheses associate a different pair of numbers.

2. H (3 × 7) + (6 × 7) The multiplication is distributed between the numbers 3 and 6.

3. A 5 + 13 and 13 + 5 The 5 and 13 have moved or commuted to different positions.

4. G (10 × 6) × 11 and 10 × (6 × 11) The parentheses associate a different pair of numbers.

5. A 81 × (9 + 1) The multiplication distributed over the 9 and 1 is brought together.

6. J 9 + 35 = 35 + 9 The 9 and 35 move or commute to different positions.

7. D (15 + 5) × 3 = (15 × 3) + (5 × 3) The multiplication can either be combined or distributed between the 15 and 5.

8. G Associative Property This shows the parentheses associating different pairs of numbers.

Lesson 9 Practice (page 25)

1. D 5 is not a factor of 12, but 1 × 12, 2 × 6, and 3 × 4 all equal 12.

2. H 32 ÷ 4 = 8

3. C 12 × 6 = 72

4. F 7 × 3 = 21

5. B 4 and 30 are not factors of 45, but 1 × 45, 3 × 15, and 5 × 9 all equal 45.

6. J 15 × 6 = 90

7. D 5 × 5 = 25

8. F 47 × 3 = 141

TABE Review: Numbers and Number Operations (pages 26–27)

1. B 2.6 is the same as $2\frac{6}{10}$. This may be reduced to $2\frac{3}{5}$. [Equivalent Form]

2. F 10% is the same as 0.10. [Percent]

3. C Divide 600 by 2, so the scale is 1 inch = 300 miles. [Ratio and Proportion]

4. G The distance from north to south is $\frac{2}{3}$ of the distance from east to west $\left(\frac{2000}{3000}\right)$. On the smaller section, the distance from east to west will be 1500 miles. [Ratio and Proportion]

5. D 0.25 is the same as $\frac{25}{100}$. This may be reduced to $\frac{1}{4}$. [Equivalent Form]

6. H There are 7 people living on each square mile of land (14 ÷ 2). To find the number of people living on 10 square miles of land multiply 10 × 7 = 70. [Ratio and Proportion]

7. A 0.30 is the same as $\frac{30}{100}$. This may be reduced to $\frac{6}{20}$. [Equivalent Form]

8. H $\frac{3}{12} = \frac{1}{4}$, which is the same as 1 inch = 4 feet. [Ratio and Proportion]

9. B Multiply 5.60 × 0.07, which is 0.39 tax on each dozen. The total cost of a dozen is $5.99 ($5.60 + 0.39). The cost of 2 dozen is $11.98 ($5.99 × 2). [Percent]

10. H Multiply 1600 × 0.20 to find how much less they'll weigh in a lean year. They will weigh 1280 pounds (1600 − 320). Multiply this weight by 5 to find the answer of 6400 pounds. [Percent]

11. A 75% is the same as $\frac{75}{100}$. This may be reduced to $\frac{3}{4}$. [Percent]

12. G 60 ÷ 80 = 0.75. This is the same as 75%. If they won 75%, they lost 25% of their games (100 − 75). [Percent]

13. A Regrouping parentheses illustrates the Associative property. [Operational Properties]

14. H 1, 2, 3, 5, 6, 10, 15, and 30 are all factors of 30, but 4, 8, and 12 are not. [Factors, Multiples, and Divisibility]

Lesson 10 Practice (page 29)

1. B In 1991, the lines for men's and women's sports participation are farthest apart.

2. J During this time period, there was an increase of about 10,000 women from the last period.

3. C The bar showing housing is the highest for this age group.

4. F The bar for food is about half as high as the bar for housing for this age group.

Lesson 11 Practice (page 31)

1. B Bulgur wheat has 25.6 grams of fiber.

2. J Clarksdale has the most restaurants.

3. C Find the average by adding 68 + 97 + 35 + 80 + 75 = 355, divide by 5 = 71. 71 rounds down to 70.

4. H Nashville scored 70 points.

5. D Ottawa has scored 80 points and Minnesota has scored 90 points. Together they have scored 170 points (90 + 80).

6. J Minnesota has scored 90 points and Nashville has scored 70 points (90 − 70 = 20).

1. **A** Mercury, Venus, and Mars have less mass than Earth. B is not covered by the data. According to the data, C and D are not true.

2. **J** The table shows data about the distance of planets in the solar system from the Sun. It does not include information about the other choices.

3. **A** There are 3 planets with less mass than Earth and 4 planets with more mass than Earth. The data does not include information about C. According to the data, B and D are not true.

4. **G** Alex's science grades improved each month. No information is given about F and H. According to the data, J is not true.

5. **D** The table shows changes in Alex's grades in science and history. No information is given about A, B, and C.

6. **G** The data shows Alex's science grades improved and his history grades got worse. According to the data, H and J are not true. The data does not give information about Alex's overall grades.

1. **A** The population of different states is most appropriately displayed on a bar graph. B and D are most appropriately displayed on a line graph; C on a circle graph.

2. **H** The percentages of voters are most appropriately displayed on a circle graph. F is most appropriately displayed on a bar graph; G and J on line graphs.

3. **D** The changing height of a an airplane is most appropriately displayed on a line graph. A and C are most appropriately displayed on bar graphs; B on a line graph.

4. **G** A circle graph is most appropriate.

5. **C** The growth of a bean plant is most appropriately shown on a line graph.

6. **G** The percentages of people who prefer different radio stations is most appropriately shown on a circle graph.

7. **D** The height of a rocket is most appropriately shown on a line graph.

8. **H** A bar graph is the most appropriate.

1. **A** A bar graph shows the number of books read by each student. [Appropriate Data Display]

2. **G** A line graph shows the change in number of books read by her class over a period of time. [Appropriate Data Display]

3. **A** Travel showed the greatest increase from year 4 to year 5. [Graphs]

4. **H** $27,500 + $35,000 + $40,000 + $45,000 = $147,500, or about $150,000. [Graphs]

5. **B** Find year 4 and list the expenses from least to greatest. [Graphs]

6. **G** Less is spent on travel in the fourth year than the second year. [Graphs]

7. **C** The graph shows elevation including maximum altitude. [Conclusions from Data]

8. **F** Round each number to the nearest ten and add: $290 + $220 + $330 + $200 + $270 + $250 + $150 = $1710 ÷ 7 = 244.3, which is rounded to $240. [Charts]

9. **B** $400 × 0.04 = $16 tax, which is added to $400. $400 + $16 = $416 [Charts]

10. **G** A line graph shows change over time. [Appropriate Data Display]

11. **A** Mining products make up the smallest percentage of imports. [Charts]

12. **G** 30% + 27% + 7% = 64% [Charts]

1. **D** When the numbers of barrels of oil are arranged from least to greatest, 500 million is the number in the middle.

1. **B** People who respond to an Internet survey are not a random sample.

2. **F** People at different voting locations best reflect all the voters.

3. **D** Students chosen from a list of all students make a random sample.

4. **F** Pencils that fail a quality control test are not a random sample.

5. **A** Customers at a different store do not represent the store's customers.

6. **G** People at one candidate's rally are not a random sample.

7. **C** Snowflakes from different storms make a random sample.

8. **H** Employees chosen from the payroll list make a random sample.

1. **C** Students chosen from a list of all students make a random sample. [Sampling]

2. **F** Olympic athletes may not represent all people. [Sampling]

3. **A** 1,920 is the total of the populations divided by 4. [Probability and Statistics]

4. **G** People selected randomly from phone directories make a random sample. [Sampling]

5. **B** $2.30 is a number in the middle of the range of prices on the table. [Probability and Statistics]

6. **H** Random samples from the stores will best represent the Snorgols being sold. [Sampling]

7. **B** $11 million is a number in the middle of the range of revenues on the graph. [Sampling]

8. G A good estimate should be based on the data already known. [Probability and Statistics]

1. C 60 seconds is 3 times as long as 20 seconds. Multiply 6×3 for the answer of 18 envelopes.

2. F $2 \times 3 = \underline{6}$, $6 \times 3 = \underline{18}$, $18 \times 3 = \underline{54}$, $54 \times 3 = \underline{162}$. You will never get the number 52.

3. D Each input number is divided by 5. $40 \div 5 = 8$.

4. H Sound travels 350 meters per second ($700 \div 2$). In 10 seconds, it would travel 3,500 meters (350×10).

5. A $6 \times 4 - 2 = 22$

6. G The pattern is $+ 400$ and then $+ 500$. If it increases by 600 between 1980 and 2000, there will be 1800 ($1,200 + 600$) billion miles traveled.

1. D If Clark can buy 4 pencils for $1.00, he can buy 5 times as many for $5.00. $4 \times 5 = 20$.

2. F If you substitute 20 for b, $20 + 5 = 25$.

3. B There are 12 months in a year, and $27.44 is taken from Barbara's pay check each month. (12)($27.44) or $12 \times \$27.44$ equals the amount Barbara will pay in Medicare tax for the year.

4. H If you multiply the number of fans per game (8,184) $\times$ 82, you will find the total number of fans for the season. 30% is equal to 0.30. The total number of fans multiplied by 0.30 will give you an estimate of the number of hot dogs sold.

5. A You know there are 60 minutes in an hour. There are five 12-minute periods in an hour ($60 \div 12 = 5$). By multiplying 3×5, you find the number of miles Renee can run in an hour.

6. G Dividing $4,011 by $3.00 gives the number of visitors for the week. Since there are 7 days in a week, dividing this result by 7 gives the average number of visitors to the lighthouse each day.

7. B $38 - 6 = 32$

1. C $800 is greater than Pat's earnings, so the wide part of the inequality points to $800.

2. F Since t is greater than 15, the wide part of the inequality points to t.

3. B $x - 4 + 4 < 10 + 4$, so $x < 14$.

4. G $2w$ represents the weight of the two suitcases, so $2w$ is less than 30 kg.

5. B The time it takes Andre to run 1 mile is represented by s. So $3s$ represents the time it takes to run 3 miles.

6. G $3t$ represents the number of tickets times the price of a ticket, so $3t$ is greater than $1,250.

7. D The table says vitamin D in the health bar is more than 200%.

8. H The table says that sodium in the health bar is less than 1%.

1. B At 3 cookies per dollar, y is the greatest number of cookies Sasha can buy with $5.00 dollars. [Equations]

2. H The sum of 15 and 5 is 20, and 20 is less than 25.

3. A First change $\frac{1}{2}$ to $\frac{2}{4}$. Then add $\frac{1}{4} + \frac{2}{4} + \frac{3}{4} = \frac{6}{4}$ or $1\frac{1}{2}$. [Applied Algebra]

4. F First divide the $8.00 Billy had to spend by the cost of 3 donuts ($2.00). $8 \div 2 = 4$. Now the equation $3 \times 4 = n$ may be used to find n, the number of donuts Billy bought. [Equations]

5. A She plays tennis 2 hours a day, 3 days a week. [Equations]

6. J $n = 35 - 20$; $n = 15$ [Number Sentences]

7. B The equation shows how many grapefruits Nina can buy for $1.00 (4), times the number of dollars she has (3), which equals the number of grapefruits she can buy for $3.00. Nina has $3.00 to spend, not $4.00 (option A). The amount of money Nina has altogether is not part of the problem or the equation (option C). The amount of money Nina has to spend on grapefruits is only <u>part</u> of the question (option D). [Equations]

8. F Write the information as a proportion. The recipe calls for 10 ounces of chicken for 6 people, or $\frac{10}{6}$. You need to find out how many ounces of chicken feed 12 people, or $\frac{n}{12}$. $\frac{n}{12} = \frac{10}{6}$, or $n = \frac{10}{6} \times 12$. [Equations]

9. C $4 \times 2 \times \square = 40$. $\square = 40 \div 8 = 5$. [Missing Element]

10. J $7 \times 2 = \underline{14}$. $14 \times 2 = \underline{28}$. $28 \times 2 = \underline{56}$. $56 \times 2 = \underline{112}$. Vick will <u>never</u> get 49. [Functions and Patterns]

11. C The rule is $\frac{1}{2} \times$ the "Input" number = the "Output" number. The missing "Output" number is $\frac{1}{2} \times 50 = 25$. [Functions and Pattern]

12. G Use $5 + 3 + \square = 10$. This becomes $8 + \square = 10$. Then $10 - 8 = 2$ red pens. [Applied Algebra]

13. D The distance the plane flew in 6 hours is greater than 85×6.

14. H Use 5×20 to show the number of seeds. Because 70% is equal to 0.70, the equation becomes $(5 \times 20) \times 0.70$ to find the number of plants expected. [Applied Algebra]

1. D Bumblebees are small, so millimeters are an appropriate unit.

2. F Ten million millimeters is more conveniently stated as 10 kilometers.

3. A Bathtubs are large enough so that gallons are an appropriate unit.

4. F Paperclips are light, so grams are an appropriate unit.

5. B The distance of 63,360 inches is more conveniently stated as 1 mile.

6. H The volume of a house is many cubic meters, but much smaller than a cubic kilometer.

7. B The distance between baseball bases is large enough to be measured in feet, but not in miles.

8. H One hundred million milligrams is more conveniently stated as 100 kilograms.

Lesson 20 Practice (page 55)

1. A Add 6:10 + 6:20 = 12:30, or $12\frac{1}{2}$ hours.

2. G Des Moines is in the Central Time Zone, so it is 1 hour earlier in Des Moines than it is in Columbus, which is in the Eastern Time Zone.

Lesson 21 Practice (page 57)

1. D Add 96 + 83 + 92 + 87 = 358 feet.

2. F If the measure from north to south is 280 miles, and the measure from east to west is 360, the perimeter is 280 + 280 + 360 + 360 = 1280 miles.

3. B Since a soccer field is a rectangle, find the perimeter by adding 361 + 361 + 246 + 246 = 1214 feet.

4. H Each side of a square is equal. 6 inches × 4 = 24 inches.

5. D Since a triangle has 3 sides, add 12 + 13 + 20 = 45 inches.

6. F Add 7 + 3 + 8 + 12 + 1 + 9 = 40 yards.

Lesson 22 Practice (page 59)

1. B To find the area, multiply 8 feet × 10 feet = 80 square feet.

2. F The town measures 8 miles × 4 miles = 32 square miles. 32 square miles ÷ 2 square-mile-section = 16 sections.

3. A 96 inches = 8 feet. 32 square feet ÷ 8 feet = 4 feet.

4. J 24 inches × 36 inches = 2 feet × 3 feet = 6 square feet.

5. B 48 inches × 60 inches = 4 feet × 5 feet = 20 square feet. Option A is 60 square feet, option C is 63 square feet, and option D is 70 square feet.

6. G 48 inches × 120 inches = 4 feet × 10 feet = 40 square feet. Sandra will need 1 bag to cover 30 square feet, plus a second bag to cover the remaining 10 square feet.

7. D To find the area, multiply 8 centimeters × 9 centimeters = 72 sq. cm.

Lesson 23 Practice (page 61)

1. C 30 ÷ 2 = 15 problems per hour

2. H 2,000 ÷ 5 = 400 miles per minute

3. A $3 \div 7 = \frac{3}{7}$ centimeters per day

4. J $5° \div 10 = \frac{1}{2}$ degree per hour

5. B $25 \div 2\frac{1}{2} = 10$ loaves per hour

6. F 500 ÷ 2 = 250 miles per hour

7. C 70 million ÷ 2 = 35 million gallons per minute

8. G 10 ÷ 5 = 2 birds per minute × 60 = 120 birds per hour

Lesson 24 Practice (page 63)

1. A The sum of the angles in a triangle is 180°. Add 81° + 43° = 124°. Then subtract 180° − 124° = 56°.

2. H Add the sum of the two known angles: 36° + 70° = 106°. Then subtract 180° − 106° = 74 degrees.

3. B Add the sum of the two known angles: 32° + 59° = 91°. Then subtract 180° − 91° = 89 degrees.

4. G Add the sum of the two known angles: 21° + 76° = 97°. Then subtract 180° − 97° = 83 degrees.

TABE Review: Measurement (pages 64–65)

1. A The amount, 6 centimeters, divided by the time, 3 hours, gives the rate, 2 centimeters per hour. [Rate]

2. F Regroup by adding 60 minutes to 00:05, and subtracting 1 hour from 9:00. 8:65 − 7:15 = 1:50. [Time]

3. B Meters is the appropriate unit. Centimeters are too small a unit for this measurement. Kilometers and miles are much too large for this measurement. [Appropriate Units]

4. J The rectangle's perimeter is 5 + 10 + 5 + 10 = 30 centimeters. [Perimeter]

5. A 12 feet × 11 feet = 132 square feet. [Area]

6. G The front side of the block is 2 × 4 = 8 square inches. [Area]

7. B Since a triangle has 180°, 180° − 30° − 60° = 90°. [Angle Measurements]

8. G Regroup by adding 60 minutes to 00:07 and regroup by subtracting 1 hour from 11:00. 10:67 − 6:55 = 4:12. [Time]

9. A Bus 611 takes 3 hours and 20 minutes. [Time]

10. H Bus 823 leaves at 9:15 a.m. Yolanda has to leave the house 45 minutes before this. 9:15 − 0:45 = 8:30. [Time]

11. B 100 ÷ 4 = 25 yards per hour [Rate]

12. F Butterflies are small, so inches are an appropriate unit. [Appropriate Units]

13. D 1,200 ÷ 3 = 400 pages per hour [Rate]

Lesson 25 Practice (page 67)

1. C The rectangle can be folded vertically or horizontally or turned a half turn.

2. F The square can be folded diagonally, but turns make it look different.

3. D The triangle cannot be folded or turned without looking different.

4. H Circles can be folded or turned without looking different.

5. C The arrow can be folded vertically or horizontally or turned a half turn.

6. H The pentagon can be folded from each corner or turned a part turn.

7. D The quadrilateral cannot be folded or turned without looking different.

8. G The parallelogram can be turned a half turn.

Lesson 26 Practice (page 69)

1. D An 8-sided figure is an octagon.

2. F A parallelogram has exactly 2 sets of parallel lines.

3. B A 5-sided figure is a pentagon.

4. J A rectangle is a parallelogram. None of the other options list figures that fit the definition of a parallelogram.

5. C A rectangle has exactly two pair of parallel lines. Option A has 4 pairs of parallel lines. Options B and D have no pairs of parallel lines.

6. H A square is the only quadrilateral listed in the answer choices.

Lesson 27 Practice (page 71)

1. C The original figure was a rectangular prism, which is cut to make a rectangular prism and a cube.

2. F Earth is a sphere.

3. B The oatmeal container is a cylinder.

4. F The figure contains a cube and a rectangular prism.

5. C This figure is a rectangular pyramid.

6. H Options F, G, and J are not true statements.

Lesson 28 Practice (page 73)

1. D The diagonals divide the square into four triangles.

2. H Three rows of 3 squares makes 9 squares.

3. B The circle is bigger than a 1-square-inch square and smaller than a 4-square-inch square.

4. J The faces of a cube are 6 squares.

5. B The long side is longer than the other sides, but shorter than the other sides combined.

6. H The shape with two circles at its ends is a cylinder.

7. D The straight line is the shortest path.

8. F The 3-foot length is divided into 1-foot lengths, and the width does not change.

Lesson 29 Practice (page 75)

1. D Lines p and r cross but do not make a square corner.

2. G Lines s and t make a square corner, so they are perpendicular.

3. B Lines p and t do not cross, so they are parallel.

4. F Lines f and g do not cross, so they are parallel.

5. B Lines f and e make a square corner, so they are perpendicular.

6. J Lines e and g make a square corner, so they are perpendicular.

Lesson 30 Practice (page 77)

1. C The sum of the angles in a triangle is 180°. Add the sum of the two known angles: 49° + 65° = 114°. Then subtract 180° − 114° = 66°.

2. J This triangle has three equal sides.

3. C Triangle 5 is the only triangle in the figure with an obtuse angle.

4. H If it is equilateral, all three sides are equal, so all the angles must be equal. 60° × 3 = 180°.

Lesson 31 Practice (page 79)

1. C The upper-left corner is 1 unit right and 5 units up.

2. F The lower-right corner is 5 units right and 3 units up.

3. C There are 8 squares of the grid inside the rectangle.

4. G The lower-right corner is 6 units right and 1 unit up.

5. D The upper-left corner is 1 unit right and 6 units up.

6. H The bottom of the triangle is 6 − 1 = 5 units long.

Lesson 32 Practice (page 81)

1. B Path A has arrows at both ends, so it represents a line.

2. H Path B has an arrow at only one end, so it represents a ray.

3. A The ray and line meet at a point.

4. H Path W has an arrow at only one end, so it represents a ray.

5. B Path V has an arrow at both ends, so it represents a line.

6. J The line W and ray V do not cross.

Lesson 33 Practice (page 83)

1. A A is a mirror image of the original parallelogram.

2. G B is a quarter-turn of the original parallelogram.

3. D C is an enlargement of the original parallelogram.

4. G X is a quarter-turn of the original trapezoid.

5. A Y can be made by a half-turn or be a mirror image.

6. H Z is identical to the original trapezoid in a new position.

TABE Review: Geometry and Spatial Sense (pages 84–85)

1. C Because there is an odd oval at the top of this group, it does not have a horizontal line that makes it symmetrical. All the others do have a horizontal line of symmetry. [Symmetry]

2. F A rotation will bring the top polygon to look exactly like this one. The other choices are shaped differently. [Transformations]

3. D An equilateral triangle is a triangle with all 3 sides the same length. [Triangles]

4. H Two sides of this figure are not parallel. [Plane Figures]

5. C $180 - (62 + 37) = 180 - 99 = 81$ degrees. [Angles]

6. H An isosceles triangle has 2 equal sides. [Triangles]

7. C The lower-left corner is 3 units over and 1 unit up. [Symmetry]

8. H One of the angles is a right angle. [Triangles]

9. B This figure is a cube. [Solid Figures]

10. G The triangle is rotated a quarter turn. [Transformations]

Lesson 34 Practice (page 87)

1. D The north side of the yard measures 96 feet. $96 \div 6 = 16$ sections of fencing needed.

2. J From Miami to Jacksonville to Atlanta is 723 miles.

3. C It is 50° at 12 a.m. and 75° at 4 p.m. $75° - 50° = 25°$.

4. J It is 55° at 6 a.m. and 70° at 12 p.m. $70° - 55° = 15°$.

Lesson 35 Practice (page 89)

1. D Since each bag is enough for 2 cakes, they will need 5 bags for 10 cakes. $5 \times \$2.99$ per bag = $14.95.

2. G Divide $3.1 \div 0.62$ to find that 5 kilometers were run.

3. C Add all the expenses ($1086.41) and subtract from Clark's salary ($1978.64).

4. H Divide $3.7 \div 0.62 = 5.97$ km.

5. B First multiply $2 \times \$12.75 = \$25.50$. This is subtracted from $40.00 to find the change of $14.50.

6. F If each roll will finish 3 of the twelve windows, 4 rolls are needed. Multiply $4 \times \$9.53$.

Lesson 36 Practice (page 91)

1. B Change $23\frac{1}{2}$ to $\frac{47}{2}$. Multiply this by 3: $\frac{47}{2} \times \frac{3}{1} = \frac{141}{2} = 70\frac{1}{2}$ pounds.

2. J First find the number of square feet by multiplying. $23\frac{1}{2} \times 15 = \frac{47}{2} \times \frac{15}{1} = \frac{705}{2}$. To find the number of tiles needed, divide. $\frac{705}{2} \div 2\frac{1}{2} = \frac{705}{2} \div \frac{5}{2} = \frac{705}{2} \times \frac{2}{5} = \frac{1410}{10}$. Simplify to 141 tiles needed to tile the ceiling.

3. C Multiply $1\frac{1}{2} \times 2 = 3$ pounds of ground beef.

4. H Divide $\frac{1}{2} \div 2 = \frac{1}{4}$ cup of breadcrumbs.

TABE Review: Computation in Context (page 92–93)

1. D Multiply. $80 \times 0.35 = \$28$ shipping charge. This is added to the $80 for a total of $108. [Decimals in context]

2. G Subtract $12 from $120 for the $12 discount. The shipping is based on $108 \times 0.20 = \$21.60$. Added to $108, the total is $129.60. [Decimals in context]

3. B Divide 9 by $\frac{3}{4}$. This is done by $\frac{9}{1} \times \frac{4}{3} = \frac{36}{3} = 12$ breaks on the hike. [Fractions in context]

4. G Multiply $\frac{140}{1} \times \frac{1}{2} = 70$ decibels. [Fractions in context]

5. A Multiply $100 \times .20 = 20$ decibels. This is added to 100 decibels for a level of 120 decibels. [Decimals in context]

Lesson 37 Practice (page 95)

1. C Divide $60 \div 10 = 6$ families per square mile.

2. G $\frac{3}{10} = 0.30$, which falls between $\frac{1}{4}$ (0.25) and $\frac{1}{3}$ (0.33).

3. C Multiply $5 \times 3 = 15$ miles per week. Remove the 0 in 20 to simplify the problem. Multiply $15 \times 2 = 30$. Then put back the 0 from 20 to get 300.

4. F Divide. $13 \div 4 = 3.25$, which is about 3 inches.

Lesson 38 Practice (page 97)

1. D First round the 3-digit dollar amounts to the nearest 100: $198.32 rounds to $200.00; $102.15 rounds to $100.00. Round the 2-digit dollar amounts to the nearest 10: $25.04 rounds to $30.00; $24.89 rounds to $20.00; and $23.44 rounds to $20.00. Add the rounded numbers $200 + 100 + 30 + 20 + 20 = 370$. Next, round the amount Isaac earns per month: $1,654.90 rounds to $1,700.00 Subtract. $1,700 - \$370.00 = \$1,330.00$

2. F When rounded to the nearest whole number, 5.985 is 6, and when rounded to the nearest tenth, it is the same number.

3. A When rounded to the nearest whole number, 1.973 is 2. When rounded to the nearest tenth, it is also 2.

Lesson 39 Practice (page 99)

1. C First round $198.99 to $200. $200 \times 20\% = \$200 \times 0.2 = \$40$. $200 + $ 40 = $240.

2. H One dozen is 12. Round 19 to 20. Multiply $20 \times 12 = 240$, which can be rounded to 250.

3. C First $62.80 can be rounded to $60.00. 25% of this amount can be found by multiplying $60 \times 0.25 = 15$. This is subtracted from $60.00 for an estimated amount of $45.00.

4. J Round all the numbers to the nearest 100. Add and divide by 7. The result, 142.9, can be rounded to 140.

1. B Multiply $20 \times 30 = 600$. [Reasonableness of Answer]

2. F Rounded to the nearest ten thousand, 158,047 is 160,000 [Rounding]

3. A Round $41.25 to $40. Next multiply $40 \times 0.10 = $4 drop per share. This leaves a new price of $36 ($40 − $4). [Rounding]

4. F Round $1.69 to $2, $2.29 to $2 and $1.29 to $1. Add $2 + 2 + 1 = 5$. Multiply $5 \times 0.20 = 1 = \$1.00$. [Rounding]

5. B $\frac{4}{10} = 0.40$, which is between $\frac{1}{3}$ (0.33) and $\frac{1}{2}$ (0.50). [Reasonableness of Answer]

6. G Because she can run a half mile in 4 minutes, and there are 4 half miles in 2 miles, multiply $4 \times 4 = 16$ minutes to run 2 miles [Estimation]

7. C Round 18% to 0.20 and $89.95 to $90. Multiply $90 \times 0.20 = \$18$. [Estimation]

8. H When rounded to the nearest whole number, 4.951 is 5; and when rounded to the nearest tenth, it is the same number. [Rounding]

9. D Round $1,858.46 to $1,900.00, $201.36 to 200, $109.32 to $100, $27.54 to $30, $22.11 to $20.00, and $34.17 to $30.00. Add the rounded numbers $200 + 100 + 30 + 20 + 30 = 380$. Round 380 to 400. Subtract $1,900 − 400 = \$1,500$ left. [Estimation]

10. G Round 147 square feet to 150. Then divide $150 \div 10$ (the number of square feet covered by one bag) = 15 bags needed. [Estimation]

11. C Round $159.95 to $160. Multiply $160 \times 0.25 = 40$. Subtract $160 − 40$ to get the sale price of a bicycle: $120. [Estimation]

Lesson 40 Practice (page 103)

1. B First calculate how many CDs were sold on Friday and Saturday. Then $\frac{2}{3}$ of that number is the number sold on Saturday.

2. H Subtracting $3 \times \$8$, $6, and $2 \times \$3$ from $48 gives the amount for 3 drinks. Dividing that number by 3 gives the amount for one drink.

3. A If the mean of 8 grades is 83, then the total of the grades is 8×83. Subtracting 575 from that product gives the last grade.

4. G Finding the measure of the third angle leads to finding the total of the two angles.

5. A The total number of pets equals $3\frac{1}{2}$ times the number of students.

6. F The plane's speed is the distance divided by the time in the air. The time in the air is $8 − 2 − 1.5$.

Lesson 41 Practice (page 105)

1. C The number of seats in each row is needed to find the number of people the arena can seat.

2. F The total number of tickets sold is needed to find out how many were sold per performance.

3. A The first step in finding the average height is to add the height of the three buildings. You need the height of the Sears Tower.

4. H The cost of the buns is needed.

5. C The number of Saturn's known moons is needed to find the total number of moons for the three planets.

6. G The number of refugees who entered Canada is needed to find the total number of refugees for both the United States and Canada.

7. B The number of Ted's friends is needed to solve this problem.

8. G The length of the phone call is needed to find the cost of the call.

Lesson 42 Practice (page 107)

1. B If 5 cartons cost $5 each, then the total spent would be $25.

2. J All probabilities range from 0 to 100%.

3. C The mean of a set of numbers is always between the minimum and the maximum.

4. G The solution to an inequality (with positive numbers) will have a sign pointing in the same direction as the original.

5. B The total amount saved over 10 weeks is $10 \times \$10$.

6. F $200 \div 8 = 25$ miles per hour.

TABE Review: Problem Solving (pages 108–109)

1. B Kristen's solution is not reasonable because replacing x with 14 does not result in 11. [Evaluate Solutions]

2. G Randy's solution is not reasonable because substituting 10 for x results in $43 > 7$. Many numbers are not included in Randy's solution. [Evaluate Solutions]

3. B The number of guests times the number of apples per guest will equal the number of apples Jose should buy. [Missing, Extra Information]

4. G Multiplying 150 by $\frac{2}{3}$ will tell how many postcards Dan has, and multiplying by 2 will tell how many Keiko has. [Solve Problems]

5. D The sale price is the normal price less a discount. It is not reasonable for the sale price to be higher. [Evaluate Solutions]

6. F Since the chorus increases by half every year, finding the number of members last year is the first step towards finding the number of members this year. [Solve Problems]

7. C The number of pages Emily read is the total of the number of pages in each book. [Missing, Extra Information]

8. F The total revenue equals the average price of the tickets times the number of tickets sold. [Missing, Extra Information]

9. C The mean describes all the numbers, so it should be between the extreme numbers in any set of data. [Evaluate Solutions]

10. J Since Ramona spent $25 for 3 magazines, the price per magazine should be $\frac{1}{3}$ of $25. [Evaluate Solutions]

11. B If Mr. Hermez drove 80 miles per hour for 10 hours, he would have driven 800 miles. Since he only drove 400 miles, his solution is not reasonable. [Evaluate Solutions]

Performance Assessment Applied Math (pages 110–121)

A. C The sequence is made up of odd numbers 3, 5, 7, 9, 11

1. D $6 \times 3 = 18$; $18 \times 2 = 36$; $36 \times 2 = 72$; $72 \times 2 = 144$; $144 \times 2 = 288$. You will never get 96. [Functions and Patterns]

2. H Interviewing students at the school entrance produces a random sample. [Sampling]

3. B This number is 403. [Recognize numbers]

4. J $r + 5 - 5 = 25 - 5$ [Expressions and Equations]

5. C $40,000 was taken in at the Giants–Brewers game and $20,000 was taken in at the Braves–Marlins Game. $40,000 is two times $20,000. [Graphs]

6. H If you know the number of students each row can seat, you can multiply that by the number of rows to find the number of students the gym can seat. [Pre-Solution]

7. B First multiply $350 \times 0.06 = $21. Then add $350 + $21 = $371.00 for the new price. [Percents in Context]

8. F The upper-left corner is 3 units over and 3 units up. [Coordinate Geometry]

9. A Add $235.04 + $117.52 + $29.38 = $381.94 [Decimals in context]

10. F As a decimal, 1% is the same as 0.01 [Percents in Context]

11. D The total of state income tax each month ($37.29) is multiplied by the number of months in a year (12) [Equations]

12. H Round his income to $2,000 and his total deductions to $400. His net monthly income is found by $2,000 − $400 = $1,600. [Rounding]

13. B Divide $3 \div 2 = 1\frac{1}{2}$. 1 inch $= 1\frac{1}{2}$ feet. [Ratio and Proportion]

14. F 36 inches = 3 feet. This is $1\frac{1}{2}$ times as high as the original chest. Multiply the length of 3 feet $\times 1\frac{1}{2} = 4\frac{1}{2}$ feet, which is equal to 54 inches. Multiply the width of 2 feet $\times 1\frac{1}{2} = 3$ feet, which is equal to 36 inches. [Ratio and Proportion]

15. D Multiply. $3 \times $12.95 = 38.85. Then multiply $38.85 \times 0.06 = 2.33 tax. The total cost of the paneling is $38.85 + $2.33 = $41.18. [Percents in Context]

16. G The area of the bottom is 2 x 3 = 6 square feet. [Area]

17. A There are 4 computer terminals. This is multiplied by 7 minutes: $4 \times 7 = 28$ minutes. This is about $\frac{1}{2}$ hour. [Estimation]

18. H Circumference is the distance around the outside of a circle. [Parts of a Circle]

19. B $\frac{1}{2}$ is the largest fraction. [Comparison]

20. J This is a right triangle. [Triangles]

21. B There are 9 sections. If 3 of the sections are devoted to native animals, this is $\frac{1}{3}$ of the sections. [Fractional part]

22. G Since $1 \times 2 \times 5 = 10$, $x = 5$. [Expressions and Equations]

23. A 0.910 is greater than 0.905 and less than 0.916. [Comparison]

24. J $11 \times 2 = 22$; $22 - 5 = 17$ [Functions and Patterns]

25. B This five-sided figure is a pentagon. [Plane Figures]

26. F The distance around Stone Memorial is 3.6 miles. The distance around Pine Meadow is 4.8 miles. $\frac{3.6}{4.8} = \frac{3}{4}$. [Fractional Part]

27. B Divide $4.2 \div 0.62 = 6.77$ kilometers [Decimals in Context]

28. G 4.8 is equal to $4\frac{8}{10}$. [Equivalent Form]

29. B Each mile takes 40 minutes to hike. It is 3.6 miles around Russian Bear. $3.6 \times 40 = 144$ minutes. $144 \div 60 = 2$ hours 24 minutes. [Time]

30. F Similar figures are the same shape but can differ in size. [Similarity]

31. A 129,612 is rounded to 130,000 when rounded to the nearest thousand. [Rounding]

32. J 8.973 is rounded to 9 when rounded to the nearest whole number and to the nearest tenth. [Rounding]

33. B 3 feet is equal to one yard, which is close to one meter. [Length]

34. F The perimeter is found by $58 + 52 + 45 + 40 = 195$ feet. [Perimeter]

35. D First divide $6 \div 2 = 3$. Then multiply $3 \times $8.75 = $26.25. [Decimals in Context]

36. H This sidewalk is 45 feet in length. $45 \div 5 = 9$ sections. [Whole numbers in Context]

37. C Interest expense is 4% of all expenses. 4% of $100,000 can be found by multiplying $100,000 $\times 0.04 = 4000. [Percents in Context]

37. C Interest expense is 4% of all expenses. 4% of $100,000 can be found by multiplying $100,000 × 0.04 = $4000. [Percents in Context]

38. H The interest expense can be found by using the equation $E =$ (total expenses for one week) × 52 × 0.04. [Equations]

39. A Add 22.2% + 4% + 9.1% = 35.3%. [Percents in Context]

40. H Multiply $70,000 by 0.3 to find the amount of the reduction, $21,000. Subtract $70,000 − $21,000 = $49,000.

41. B The temperature in Chicago increased by 11° between April and May. This was the largest increase of any city. [Graphs]

42. F New York and Chicago both had temperatures below 65° in four of the five months. [Graphs]

43. D The cities in order from least to greatest average temperatures in May are Chicago, New York, Los Angeles, Atlanta, and Houston. [Graphs]

44. H First add the temperatures in March: 40° + 50° + 70° + 74° + 65° = 299. Then divide 299 ÷ 5 = 59 with a remainder of 4. This is rounded to 60°. [Estimation]

45. D $\frac{15}{30} = \frac{1}{2}$ inch [Fractional Part]

46. H Divide 120 ÷ 30 = 4 inches. [Reasonableness of answer]

47. B Multiply $1.89 × 10 = $18.90. [Money]

48. F First find $\frac{1}{3}$ of 300 miles by multiplying

$300 \times \frac{1}{3} = 100$ miles.

They still have 200 miles to travel (300 − 100). Then divide 200 ÷ 4 = 50 miles per hour. [Fractions in Context]

49. A On the original map, 240 miles would be 8 inches (240 ÷ 30). Using a scale of 1 inch = 40 miles, 240 miles would be 6 inches on the map (240 ÷ 40). [Estimation]

50. J The triangle has been enlarged, so this is a dilation. [Transformations]